AIR FRYER

COOKBOOK FOR BEGINNERS

1000 Easy and Affordable Recipes to Fry, Bake, Grill, Roast and Seafood, vegetables with Your Air Fryer

By

DEAN JACKSON

Notice of Disclaimer:

Please keep in mind that the material in this booklet is only for educational and entertaining purposes. Every effort has been made to present accurate, up-to-date, reliable, and comprehensive information. There are no express or implied guarantees. Readers understand that the author is not providing legal, financial, medical, or professional advice. This book's material was compiled from a variety of sources. Please talk to a licensed expert before you try any of the things in this book.

As a condition of reading this document, you agree that the author is not liable for any direct or indirect damages that may arise from your use of the information in this document. This includes but is not limited to mistakes, misstatements, or omissions.

TABLE OF CONTENTS

THE AIR FRYER INTRODUCTION

T his book will teach you all you need to know about air fryers, whether you got one as a present and are unclear what to do with it, or if you're thinking about buying one.

This book has a variety of information, advice, and ideas for using an air fryer, as well as great dishes to try.

This book will demonstrate the versatility of your air fryer by showing you how to prepare a number of different meals using a wide array of ingredients. The recipes in this book are simple and straightforward to follow. Whatever you're preparing, from various sorts of meat to veggies, appetizers to desserts, your new home appliance can handle it all in the cleanest and most hygienic manner possible. To begin, what precisely is an air fryer and what does it do? These are critical questions to ask.

WHAT EXACTLY IS AN AIR FRYER AND HOW DOES IT FUNCTION?

What exactly is an air fryer and how does it function? This is a question that many customers continue to have. The name may be deceptive, since this air cooker is capable of much more than frying up diet-busting delicacies. It's up to you whether you want it baked, roasted, grilled, fried, or fried again!

You can count on us to explain how and why this vital kitchen gadget works and what it accomplishes.

Learn how the air fryer utilizes convection currents to cook your food, how it compares to other kitchen appliances, what unique functions this gadget has, and much more in the sections below.

WHAT EXACTLY IS THE FUNCTION OF A DEEP-FAT FRYER?

Air fryers, like classic fryers, pump hot air over the dish rather than immersing it in oil. Fried meals that have been prepared correctly are crispy, juicy, golden brown, and delectable.

When you use an air fryer to cook, you are using the Maillard reaction, which is a scientific concept that results in what we term "browning." High temperatures cause proteins, carbohydrates, and fibers to break down when the outside of a food item forms a crust as a consequence of drying out. All foods that are fried, roasted, or baked have a unique taste that comes from the oil that was used to make them.

An air fryer is a miniature convection oven, more specifically a compact cylindrical countertop convection oven, that cooks food quickly and evenly (try saying that three times fast).

Convection is the propensity of hot gases (or liquids) to pass one another as they move across space. Hot air, for example, rises, pushing colder air to descend as a consequence. Convection influences the weather, and it is also at work in the molten rock that drives volcanic eruptions. But you may be wondering, what does this have to do with you?

WHAT ABOUT THE COOKING EQUIPMENT?

Crisp meals may be prepared in air fryers by utilizing convection cooking, which cooks them quickly and effectively. The air fryer's heating element super-heats the air, producing natural convection currents to flow. A fan within the appliance assists in the movement of air, allowing it to circulate more quickly. The cooking basket's perforations, or holes, enable hot air to circulate freely around the food as it cooks. This increased the quantity of heat transmission from the air to the food. As a result, your dinner will be ready sooner rather than later!

IS IT SAFE TO EAT FOODS THAT HAVE BEEN AIR-FRIED?

IS RADIATION INVOLVED IN AIR FRYER COOKING?

The simple answer is no. Microwave ovens and air fryers differ in that microwaves employ electromagnetic radiation called microwaves to excite water molecules and heat the food via friction. To cook their meals, air fryers do not use any radiation.

Air fryers, on the other hand, employ a heating element similar to that found in any oven, toaster, or cooktop, which saves you money on power. The heating element generates heat when an electrical current is transformed into heat.

IS IT TRUE THAT AIR FRYERS WORK? IS IT TRUE THAT AIR FRYERS WORK?

In a previous post, we explored how air fryers work. Now you want to know whether they work, that is, if they operate the way they were advertised on television. Is it feasible that they will be able to manufacture the crispy, tasty dishes that they advertise? Is all of the hype around air fryers justified?

Air fryers are useful and efficient when used as intended and with high-quality recipes. Crispy French fries, luscious roasted fowl, air-fried vegetables, and a range of other delights are among the selections. See our air fryer cooking charts to estimate the temperature and time to cook your favorite recipes in an air fryer.

WHAT ARE THE ADVANTAGES OF USING AN AIR FRYER IN THE COOKING ENVIRONMENT?

The following are just a few of the reasons why an air fryer could be a good investment for your family:

PREPARING FOOD FOR OPTIMAL WELL-BEING

Even though everyone likes the flavor of deep-fried dishes, many individuals are unable to eat them owing to health risks. If you're aiming to lower your cholesterol or lose weight, an air fryer may be advantageous, and your doctor may approve your decision if you use one to cook. Air fryers are a healthier option that does not sacrifice taste because they use approximately 75% less oil than deep fryers.

IT'S PREPARATION TIME!

The air fryer's compact convection oven warms and cooks food more rapidly than a normal oven, resulting in crispier, more flavorful results. With less time and less waiting, you'll be able to enjoy delicious meals more quickly.

THE PREPARATION OF THE DISH INCLUDES THE USE OF GREEN INGREDIENTS.

Have you made the choice to "go green?" If so, what are your plans? When it comes to cooking, employing an air fryer may be useful in a variety of scenarios. In general, air fryers use less power because they cook food for shorter amounts of time, which means they use less total power.

SIMPLE AND BASIC IN ITS DESIGN.

Air fryers are equipped with simple controls, such as two knobs for setting frying time and temperature, or a digital display that is easy to see and use. Simply toss the food in the oil (if used), drop it in the basket, and let the air fryer take care of the rest.

When it comes to cleaning up after oneself, it is a piece of cake.

Because most air fryer baskets and pans are dishwasher safe, cleaning up after using an air fryer is simple. Furthermore, the air fryer's limited design reduces the amount of splatters and spills that occur when deep frying or pan-frying food, respectively.

SAFE

By not using the large oil vats used in conventional deep fryers, air fryers reduce the possibility of serious burns from spilt oil. Air fryers are also designed in such a way that the exterior of the appliance does not get dangerously hot to the touch when cooking.

In this part, you'll discover questions and answers to your queries.

The following are the several kinds of oils that may be used in an air fryer:

A wide variety of oils with high smoke points will function magnificently when used in your oil mister nozzle. The fact that the oil can withstand high temperatures before it is burned is a sign that it is of high value.

In addition to having a high smoke point of 570 degrees Fahrenheit, avocado oil has a particular taste that is enhanced when it is used in the kitchen. Light olive oil (468 degrees), refined coconut oil (450 degrees), and peanut oil (450 degrees) are all suitable alternatives for this use. Light olive oil is also good for this application. High-quality alternatives to olive oil include Bertolli brand oil and grape seed oil.

IS IT NECESSARY TO USE OIL IF YOU'RE COOKING IN AN AIR FRYER?

It is not necessary to use a deep fryer to prepare items that would ordinarily be cooked in an air fryer. Dishes such as fries or onion rings are coated with oil before being fried in the machine's high-circulating heat, which makes them crisp on the outside and delicate on the inside. The vast majority of recipes call for only about 1 tablespoon of oil, which should be applied with a sprayer rather than a brush to ensure even distribution.

The use of extra oil is not required for fatty dishes such as bacon or bacon fat. When it comes to leaner meats, a little oil will be required to prevent them from adhering to the pan during cooking.

Is it better to use an air fryer instead of an oven when you're cooking food?

When it comes to performance, do air fryers outperform conventional ovens?

The convection principle is used in both air fryers and in convection ovens, but the two devices are very different in how they work and how they are built.

As a result of the heated air circulated by the fan, both appliances may be able to shorten the amount of time spent cooking. According to industry standards, countertop convection ovens are typically bigger in size than air fryers. In contrast to air fryers, which can only cook between two and six meals at a time, this equipment is built for large-scale cooking.

As a result of their dishwasher-safe parts, air fryers are very easy to clean. They can be used with a wide range of different accessories.

IS THERE A VARIETY OF FOODS THAT CAN BE PREPARED IN AN AIR FRYER?

In addition, French fries, tater tots, onion rings, and hand-cut potato chips are available for purchase at the concession stand.

- Baked potatoes are a delicious side dish to serve with any meal.
- Grilled cheese sandwiches are a popular choice for lunch or dinner.
- Baked vegetables (vegetables that have been baked in the oven)
- Fresh corn on the cob is considered a delicacy in certain circles.
- Single-serving pizzas are also available on the menu.
- An empanada is a type of pastry.

Egg rolls, crab Rangoon, and spring rolls are some of the most popular appetizers in the Philippines.

- Donuts with slits in them
- Chicken is a good example of a protein that is high in protein.
- A hamburger is a kind of sandwich.
- Bacon is a delicacy.
- Fishing is a popular pastime.
- Brisket of beef

Steak? The statement is correct, and you have correctly read it. Cooking beautiful, delicate steaks in an air fryer is easy and fast, and the results are delicious.

Pizza? However, although you won't be able to fit an entire frozen pizza in there, you may reheat leftovers or make your own little pizzas out of pita or naan bread to fit the available space.

As you can see, the choices are almost limitless. If you can cook anything at home, there is a good possibility that you can cook it in your air fryer as well.

BREAD AND BREAKFAST

HARD-BOILED EGGS

Preparation time: 1 minute/Cooking time: 15 minutes/Serves 6

Preheat the oven to 300°F.

FAMILY FAVORITE VEGETARIAN, GLUTEN-FREE

You can hard-cook eggs in the air fryer, believe it or not! If you don't mind a few little black areas where the egg comes into contact with the basket, this is a lot simpler approach to cooking this delicacy.

Six huge eggs

1. Place the eggs in the air fryer basket in a single layer.
2. Bake for at least 8 minutes if you want a somewhat runny yolk, or 12 to 15 minutes if you want a firmer yolk. To discover the ideal time for your air fryer, you may need to experiment.
3. Using tongs gently remove the eggs from the air fryer and immediately set them in a dish of very cold water. Allow the eggs to stand in cold water for 5 minutes before gently cracking the shell under running water. Allow the eggs to remain for another minute or two before peeling and eating.

Suggestions for an ingredient:

- Make a large batch of eggs ahead of time for a quick and healthy breakfast. They may be stored in the refrigerator for three days. Cooked eggs should never be stored at room temperature for food safety concerns.

Cost per serving:

Calories: 63, Total fat: 4g, saturated fat: 1g, cholesterol: 164mg, sodium: 62mg, carbs: 1g, fiber: 0g, protein: 6g

Asparagus Strata

Preparation time: 12 minutes/Cooking time: 17 minutes/Serves 4

Preheat the oven to 330°F.

Vegetarian

A strata is a baked egg-topped bread, vegetable, and cheese concoction. It's a hybrid of a bread pudding and a frittata, combining the best qualities of each. You may use whatever kind of bread you have on hand for this recipe.

Ingredients:

- 6 spears of asparagus, sliced into 2-inch pieces.
- 2 whole-wheat bread slices, cut into 1/2-inch cubes.
- Four eggs
- three tablespoons whole milk
- 1/2 cups of Havarti or Swiss cheese, grated
- 2 tbsp. flat-leaf parsley, chopped
- A pinch of salt
- Freshly ground black pepper.

Method:

1. In a 6-inch baking dish, combine the asparagus spears with 1 tablespoon of water.
2. Place the pan in the air fryer basket. 3 to 5 minutes, or until crisp and tender. Remove the asparagus from the pan and set it aside to drain. Nonstick cooking spray should be sprayed on the pan.
3. Place the bread cubes and asparagus in a pan and set aside.
4. In a medium mixing bowl, combine the eggs and milk. Combine the cheese, parsley, salt, and pepper in a mixing bowl. Pour the mixture into the baking dish.
5. Bake for 11–14 minutes, or until the eggs are set and the top is beginning to brown.

A suggestion for a substitution:

Substitute other veggies for the asparagus. Vegetables from the fridge work wonderfully. In this tasty meal, use cooked peas, broccoli, green beans, or zucchini.

Cost per serving:

9g total fat, 4g saturated fat, 178mg cholesterol, 200mg sodium, 9g carbohydrate, 2g fiber, 12g protein

FRITTATA WITH SHRIMP AND RICE

Preparation time: 15 minutes/Cooking time: 15 minutes/Serves 4

Preheat the oven to 320°F.

Gluten-Free:

Use leftover rice or rice from your favorite Asian restaurant to make this meal even simpler. You may also purchase frozen rice, which can be readily thawed by pouring hot water over it.

Ingredients:

- Four eggs
- A pinch of salt
- 1/2 tsp. dried basil
- Cooking spray that is nonstick
- COOKED RIBBON 12 CUP
- 1/2 cups of cooked shrimp, chopped
- 1/2 cups of fresh baby spinach
- 1/2 cups of Monterey Jack or Cojack cheese, grated

Method:

1. In a small mixing bowl, whisk together the eggs, salt, and basil until foamy. Use nonstick cooking spray on a 6-by-6-by-2-inch baking pan.
2. In the preheated pan, combine the rice, shrimp, and spinach. Pour in the eggs and top with the cheese.
3. Bake for 14–18 minutes or until the frittata puffs up and becomes golden brown.

A suggestion for a substitution:

This recipe may be modified to suit your preferences. If you don't like shrimp, you may substitute cooked sausages or chopped cooked chicken. If you don't want to eat spinach, you can chop up some bell peppers or freeze some baby peas instead.

Cost per serving:

226 calories, 9g total fat, 4g saturated fat, 221mg cholesterol, 232mg sodium, 19g carbohydrate, 0g fiber, and 16g protein

EGGS SCOTCH

Preparation time: 15 minutes/Cooking time: 12 minutes/Serves 6

Temperature of the fryer: 370 °F

<u>Family member's favorite</u>

Scotch eggs are an English favorite that consist of a hard-cooked egg wrapped in pig sausage and deep-fried. In this recipe, you'll lighten it up by substituting chicken sausage and frying it in the air fryer. For a special breakfast, serve it with a fruit salad and cinnamon buns or muffins.

<u>Ingredients:</u>

- Six firm-boiled eggs
- 1 1/2 pound lean turkey or chicken sausage
- 3 raw eggs, separated
- 1 1/2 c. dry bread crumbs
- 1/2 cups of all-purpose flour
- Misting oil made from oil

<u>Method:</u>

1. Set aside the hard-cooked eggs after peeling them.
2. Mix together the chicken sausage, one raw egg, and 1/2 cups of the bread crumbs in a large mixing basin. Divide the dough into six equal halves and flatten each into a long oval.
3. Beat the remaining two raw eggs in a small basin.
4. Roll each hard-cooked egg in flour and wrap one of the chicken sausage pieces fully around the egg.
5. Roll the egg in flour first, then in the beaten eggs, and then in the bread crumbs to coat. Proceed with the remaining eggs in the same manner.
6. Spray the eggs with oil and arrange them in a single layer in the air fryer.
7. Air-fry for 6 minutes before turning with tongs and misting with extra oil. 5–7 minutes in the air fryer or until the chicken is well cooked and the Scotch eggs are brown.

What Did You Know?

Many supermarket shops sell hard-cooked eggs that have already been peeled! Look for them in the dairy section, and be sure to stick to the expiry dates. You can also hard-cook them in your air fryer (Hard-Cooked Eggs, here).

Cost per serving:

623 calories; 40 grams of total fat; 13 grams of saturated fat; 341 milligrams of cholesterol; 1,140 milligrams of sodium; 28 grams of carbohydrates; 2 grams of fiber; 35 grams of protein

OMELETTE IN A BREAD CUP

Preparation time: 12 minutes/Cooking time: 11 minutes/Serves 4

Preheat the oven to 330°F.

Family member's favorite

A creative spin on a breakfast favorite is to serve an omelette in a bread cup. The bread crisps and toasts, while the eggs remain moist and fluffy. You may add various things to the eggs, but bacon and cheese are a delicious savory combination.

Ingredients:

- Four crusty rolls (3-by-4-inch)
- 4 small wedges of thinly sliced Gouda or Swiss cheese.
- A dozen eggs
- 2 teaspoons heavy cream
- 1/2 tsp. dried thyme
- 3 slices of chopped precooked bacon.
- A pinch of salt
- Freshly ground black pepper.

Method:

1. Remove the tops of the rolls and use your fingers to remove the insides to form a shell with about 1/2 inches of bread left. Line the rolls with a piece of cheese, carefully pushing down to conform the cheese to the interior of the roll.
2. In a medium mixing bowl, combine the eggs and heavy cream.
3. Add the thyme, bacon, salt, and pepper to taste.
4. Over the cheese, spoon the egg mixture into the rolls.
5. Bake for 8 to 12 minutes or until the eggs are fluffy and the top is beginning to brown.

Suggestions for an ingredient:

Freeze any leftover bread to make homemade bread crumbs later. They are much superior to store-bought bread crumbs.

Cost per serving:

499 calories, 24g total fat, 9g saturated fat, 250mg cholesterol, 1,025mg sodium, 46g carbohydrate, 2g fiber, and 25g protein

MUFFINS WITH MIXED BERRIES

MAKES 8 MUFFINS IN 15 MINUTES/TIME TO COOK: 15 MINUTES

Preheat the oven to 320°F.

A Vegetarian Family Favorite

This simple recipe yields eight light and delicate muffins that the whole family will enjoy. Choose your favorite fresh berries, such as cut strawberries, blueberries, or raspberries.

Ingredients:

- 1 tablespoon flour plus 1 1/3 cup
- 2 tablespoons of baking soda.
- 1/4 cups of granulated sugar
- 2 tablespoons brown sugar
- Two eggs
- 2/3 cup whole milk
- 1/2 pound safflower oil
- 1 cup mixed fresh berries

Method:

1. Mix together the 1 1/3 cups of flour, baking powder, white sugar, and brown sugar in a medium mixing basin.
2. Combine the eggs, milk, and oil in a small mixing basin and whisk until mixed. Just combine the egg mixture with the dry ingredients.
3. Toss the mixed berries with the remaining 1 tablespoon of flour in a separate small bowl until coated. Gently fold into the batter.
4. 16 foil muffin cups may be doubled to produce 8 cups. Fill 4 cups of the air fryer with batter, about three-quarters full. Bake for 12–17 minutes, or until the muffin tops spring back when gently tapped with a finger.
5. Rep with the rest of the muffin cups and batter. Allow it to cool for 10 minutes on a wire rack before serving.

What Did You Know? Use frozen berries in this recipe, but don't defrost them beforehand. When frozen berries are thawed, the batter becomes excessively moist, and the berries may discolor the batter.

Cost per serving:

230 calories; 11 grams of total fat; 2 grams of saturated fat; 43 milligrams of cholesterol; and 26 milligrams of sodium,30g carbohydrate, 1g fiber, and 4g protein

BEIGNETS WITH CRANBERRIES

PREP TIME: 15 MINUTES/COOK TIME: 10 MINUTES/MAKES 16 BEIGNETS

Preheat the oven to 330°F.

A Vegetarian Family Favorite:

The small puffs were made famous by New Orleans' Café du Monde, which serves them with hot, freshly brewed chicory coffee. The dough for these beignets contains chopped dried cranberries, which gives them a lovely taste and color. Because this is a baking powder beignet recipe, you won't have to wait for the yeast dough to rise.

Ingredients:

- 1 1/2 pound of flour
- 2 teaspoon baking powder
- 1/4 tsp of salt
- 3 tbsp brown sugar
- 1/3 cups of dried cranberries, chopped
- 1/2 gallon buttermilk
- One egg
- 3 tbsp unsalted butter, melted

Method:

1. In a medium mixing basin, combine the flour, baking soda, salt, and brown sugar. Mix in the dried cranberries.
2. Combine the buttermilk and eggs in a small mixing dish and whisk until smooth.
3. Stir the wet ingredients into the dry ingredients just until moistened.
4. Cut the dough into 16 pieces after patting it into an 8-by-8-inch square. Lightly coat each piece with melted butter.

5. Place the pieces in the air fryer basket in a single layer, ensuring that they don't touch. Depending on the size of your air fryer basket, you may need to cook in batches. Cook, stirring occasionally, for 5–8 minutes, or until puffy and golden brown. If desired, dust the cake with powdered sugar before serving.

What Did You Know? Using unsalted butter prevents food from sticking to the air fryer basket during cooking. The salt in butter may cause dishes to clump together, which is not what you want.

Cost per serving:

76 calories; 3 grams of total fat; 2 grams of saturated fat; 16 milligrams of cholesterol; and 221 milligrams of sodium ,2g protein; 11g carbohydrate; 0g fiber

PANCAKES FROM THE NETHERLANDS

Preparation time: 12 minutes/Cooking time: 15 minutes/Serves 4

Preheat the oven to 330°F.

A Vegetarian Family Favorite

A Dutch pancake is produced with a batter that is swiftly baked over high heat so that it puffs up in the oven. When you take it out of the oven, it collapses, creating a natural well to fill with anything you want—from scrambled eggs to fresh fruits to gobs of syrup. Serve with turkey bacon and a glass of chilled orange juice.

Ingredients:

- 2 tbsp (small) unsalted butter
- Three eggs
- 1/2 cups of all-purpose flour
- 1/2 gallon of milk
- 1/2 tsp vanilla extract
- 1 1/2 cups of fresh strawberries, sliced
- 2 tbsp powdered sugar

Method:

1. Preheat the air fryer basket with a 6-by-6-by-2-inch pan in it. Heat the butter in a small saucepan until it melts.
2. Meanwhile, in a medium bowl, whisk together the eggs, flour, milk, and vanilla extract until they're all mixed together and frothy.

3. Remove the basket and pan from the air fryer with care, tilting the pan so the butter coats the bottom. Pour in the batter right away and return to the frying.
4. 12 to 16 minutes or until the pancake is puffy and golden brown.
5. Remove the pancake from the oven; it will fall. Serve immediately, topped with strawberries and powdered sugar.

A suggestion for a substitution:

This pancake may also be paired with savory ingredients. Add some crisply fried bacon, hot cooked sausage, or melted cheese to the crispy and hot pancake.

Cost per serving:

9g total fat; 5g saturated fat; 138mg cholesterol; 96mg sodium; 22g carbohydrate; 2g fiber; 7g protein

BREAD WITH MONKEYS

Time To Prepare: 7 Minutes/Time To Cook: 8 Minutes/Serves 4

Bake at 350°F.

VEGETARIAN, FAMILY FAVORITE, AND QUICK

Monkey bread is an unusual name for a breakfast delicacy with no bananas! Instead, biscuit dough is divided into pieces, brushed with butter, sugar, and spices, and baked. When the sweet bread is done baking, just pick off slices and serve them warm.

Ingredients:

- 1 refrigerated biscuit can (8 oz.)
- 1/4 cups of granulated sugar
- 3 tbsp brown sugar
- 1/2 teaspoons cinnamon powder
- 1/8 teaspoons of ground nutmeg
- 3 tbsp unsalted butter, melted

Method:

1. Open the biscuit can, divide the biscuits, and cut each biscuit into four pieces.
2. In a small dish, combine the white sugar, brown sugar, cinnamon, and nutmeg.
3. Dip each biscuit in the butter for a few seconds before rolling in the sugar mixture to coat. In a 6-by-6-by-2-inch baking pan, combine all of the ingredients.

4. 6 to 9 minutes, or until golden brown. Allow it to cool for 5 minutes before serving. When you initially start eating, be cautious since the sugar becomes really hot.

What Did You Know? The origin of the term "Monkey Bread" is lost in the annals of time. Some believe it earned its name because it resembles the

Tree of the Monkey Puzzle Perhaps the bread is "as much fun as a barrel of monkeys."

Cost per serving:

393 calories; 17 grams total fat; 8 grams saturated fat; 24 milligrams cholesterol; 787 milligrams sodium; 55 grams carbohydrates; 1 gram fiber; 5 grams protein

DOUGHNUT HOLES WITH CHOCOLATE FILLING

Preparation time: 10 minutes; cooking time: 12 minutes; yields 24 doughnut holes.

FRY 340 °F

A Vegetarian Family Favorite

Doughnut holes are the little circular puffs removed when doughnuts are made. In this scenario, you wrap each piece of biscuit dough around a chocolate chip. The chocolate interior melts when cooked, creating a delectable morning delight.

Ingredients:

- 1 can (8 counts) refrigerated biscuits
- Between 24 and 48 semisweet chocolate chips,
- 3 tbsp unsalted butter, melted
- 1/4 cups of granulated sugar

Method:

1. Each biscuit should be separated and sliced into thirds.
2. Flatten each biscuit piece slightly and fill the middle with 1 to 2 chocolate chunks. Wrap the dough tightly around the chocolate, sealing the edges securely.
3. Brush a little amount of butter into each doughnut hole and air-fry in batches for 8 to 12 minutes.
4. Sprinkle with powdered sugar after removing from the oven. Serve hot.

A tip for a variation:

Fillings for these little doughnut holes may be as imaginative as you like. Chop up candy bars or use a mix of chocolate chips and almonds. Just be careful not to overfill the dough, otherwise the holes may split while air frying.

Cost per serving:

393 calories; 17 grams total fat; 8 grams saturated fat; 24 milligrams cholesterol; 787 milligrams sodium, 5g protein; 1g fiber; 55g carbohydrate

LUNCH RECIPES

Egg Rolls with Vegetables

PREP TIME: 15 MINUTES/COOK TIME: 10 MINUTES/MAKES 8 EGG ROLLS

390°F FRYING

A Vegetarian Family Favorite

The air fryer and egg rolls are a fantastic complement. With very little oil, the covering becomes crisp and light and the contents are precisely cooked. For lunch, serve with soy or sweet-and-sour dipping sauces.

Ingredients:

- 1/2 cups of sliced mushrooms
- 1/2 cups of carrots, grated
- 1/2 cups of diced zucchini
- 2 green onions, chopped
- 2 tbsp. of low-sodium soy sauce
- 8 spring roll wrappers
- 1 tsp corn starch
- 1 egg, beaten

Method:

1. Stir together the mushrooms, carrots, zucchini, green onions, and soy sauce in a medium bowl.
2. Spread the egg roll wrappers out on a work surface. Approximately 3 tablespoons of the veggie mixture should be placed on top of each.
3. In a small mixing dish, combine the cornstarch and egg. Brush some of this mixture on the egg roll wrappers' edges. Roll the wrappers up to enclose the veggie filling. To seal the egg rolls, brush some of the egg mixture on the exterior.
4. Air-fry the egg rolls for 7 to 10 minutes, or until they are golden and crispy.

A suggestion for a substitution:

You may use spring roll wrappers for this recipe; they are thinner than egg roll wrappers and will cook faster.

Calories: 112 calories; 1 gram total fat; 0 gram saturated fat; 23 milligrams cholesterol; 417 milligrams sodium; 21 gram carbohydrate; 1 gram fiber; 4 gram protein

TOAST WITH VEGETABLES

Preparation time: 12 minutes/Cooking time: 11 minutes/Serves 4

Preheat the oven to 330°F.

Vegetarian

In this simple, healthful meal, roasted veggies are topped with toasted bread topped with creamy goat cheese. You may use whatever delicate vegetables you choose.

Root vegetables, such as potatoes or carrots, require more time to roast and should not be paired with softer foods.

Ingredients:

- 1/2 inch red bell pepper slices
- 1 cup sliced button or cremini mushrooms
- 1 small yellow squash, sliced
- 2 green onions, sliced into 1/2-inch rounds
- Misting with extra light olive oil
- 4 to 6 slices of French or Italian bread.
- 2 tablespoons softened butter
- 1/2 oz. soft goat cheese.

Method:

1. In the air fryer, combine the red peppers, mushrooms, squash, and green onions and spritz with oil. Cook for 7–9 minutes, or until the
2. Shake the basket once throughout the cooking time until the veggies are tender.
3. Set the veggies aside after removing them from the basket.
4. Spread butter on the bread and toast it in the air fryer, butter side up.
5. 2 to 4 minutes, or until golden brown.
6. Top the toasted bread with the goat cheese and veggies and serve warm.

A tip for a variation:

Drizzle the completed toasts with extra-virgin olive oil and balsamic vinegar to give them even more flavor.

Calories:

162 calories; 11 grams of total fat; 7 grams of saturated fat; 30 milligrams of cholesterol; 160 milligrams of sodium; 9 grams of carbohydrates; 2 grams of fiber; and 7 grams of protein

STUFFED MUSHROOMS IN JUMBO SIZE

Time To Prepare: 10 Minutes/Time To Cook: 20 Minutes/Serves 4

Preheat the oven to 390°F.

Vegetarian

Portobello mushrooms with a diameter of around 3 inches may typically be found in the vegetable department. These mushrooms are enormous enough (and filling enough) that one serves as a meal. Fresh rosemary adds a pleasant note to the creamy spinach filling.

Ingredients:

- 4 jumbo Portobello mushrooms
- 1 tablespoon of olive oil
- Ricotta cheese (1/4 c)
- 5 tbsp. Parmesan cheese (divided)
- 1 cup frozen chopped spinach, thawed and drained
- 1/3 pound bread crumbs
- 1/4 teaspoon minced fresh rosemary

Method:

1. Using a moist towel, wipe off the mushrooms. Remove and discard the stems.
2. Use a spoon to gently scrape out the majority of the gills.
3. Rub the olive oil into the mushrooms. Bake for 3 minutes in the air fryer basket, hollow side up. Remove the mushroom tops with care, as they will retain liquid. Remove the caps and drain the liquid.
4. Combine the ricotta, 3 tablespoons of Parmesan cheese, spinach, bread crumbs, and rosemary in a medium mixing basin.
5. Stuff the drained mushroom tops with this mixture. Add the remaining 2 tablespoons of Parmesan cheese on top. Replace the mushroom tops in the basket.
6. 4–6 minutes, or until the mixture is heated through and the mushroom caps are soft.

What Did You Know? The gills of huge mushroom caps are edible, although when cooked, they may be harsh. They are readily removed with a spoon.

Cost per serving:

117 calories; 7 grams of total fat; 3 grams of saturated fat; 10 milligrams of cholesterol; 180 milligrams of sodium,8 g carbohydrate, 1 g fiber, and 7 g protein

PITA PIZZAS WITH MUSHROOMS

Preparation time: 10 minutes/Cooking time: 5 minutes/Serves 4

Preheat the oven to 360°F.

FAST

Pita bread provides an excellent crust for a fast pizza. In the air fryer, the bread becomes crisp and crispy, while the cheese becomes bubbly and golden. This fundamental approach may be used to produce pizza with almost any cooked topping, such as meat or vegetables.

Ingredients:

- 4 pita breads (approximately 3 inches)
- 1 teaspoon olive oil
- one-quarter cup pizza sauce
- 1 jar (4 oz.) drained sliced mushrooms
- 1/2 tsp. dried basil
- Two minced green onions.
- 1 cup provolone or mozzarella cheese, grated
- 1 cup sliced grape tomatoes

Method:

1. Brush each pita with olive oil and top it with pizza sauce.
2. Sprinkle the basil and green onions over the mushrooms. Garnish with shredded cheese if desired.
3. Bake for 3–6 minutes, or until the cheese melts and begins to color.
4. Serve immediately, with the grape tomatoes on top.

A suggestion for a substitution:

Look for bottled pizza sauce in the supermarket's pasta section. Alternatively, use 3/4 cups of pasta sauce with a teaspoon of dried basil, thyme, oregano, marjoram, and cayenne pepper.

Cost per serving:

231 calories; 9 grams of total fat; 4 grams of saturated fat; 15 milligrams of cholesterol; 500 milligrams of sodium, 13g protein; 2g fiber; 25g carbohydrate

QUICHE WITH SPINACH

Preparation time: 10 minutes/Cooking time: 20 minutes/Serves 3

Preheat the oven to 320°F.

GLUTEN-FREE, VEGETARIAN

A crestless quiche is not only easier to make, but it is also less thick than the original. This dish is perfect for a quick lunch and tastes even better the following day when served cold.

Ingredients:

- Three eggs
- 1 cup frozen chopped spinach, thawed and drained
- 1/3-cup heavy cream
- 2 tablespoons honey mustard
- 1/2 cup grated Swiss or Havarti cheese
- 1/2 tsp. dried thyme
- A pinch of salt
- Freshly ground black pepper.
- Flour-based nonstick baking spray

Method:

1. In a medium mixing basin, combine the eggs. Combine the spinach, cream, honey mustard, cheese, thyme, salt, and pepper in a mixing bowl.
2. Using nonstick spray, coat a 6-by-6-by-2-inch baking pan. Fill the pan halfway with the egg mixture.
3. Bake for 18 to 22 minutes, or until the egg mixture puffs up and becomes a light golden color.
4. Allow for 5 minutes cooling before cutting into wedges to serve.

A suggestion for a substitution:

As long as the proportions remain about the same, you may substitute any cooked, leftover vegetable in this simple recipe. Cooked broccoli florets, steamed asparagus segments, or cooked mushrooms are all good additions.

Cost per serving:

203 calories; 15 grams of total fat; 8 grams of saturated fat; 199 milligrams of cholesterol; 211 milligrams of sodium, 11g protein; 6g carbohydrate; 0g fiber

FRITTERS WITH YELLOW SQUASH

Preparation time: 15 minutes/Cooking time: 7 minutes/Serves 4

FRY 340 °F

A Vegetarian Family Favorite:

Fritters are often prepared with shredded veggies, cheese, and an egg, and then fried in lard until golden and crisp. They're made with very little fat in the air fryer, yet they nevertheless have a crispy outside and a tasty, rich inside.

Ingredients:

- 1 package softened cream cheese (3 oz.)
- 1 egg, beaten
- 1/2 tsp. dried oregano
- A pinch of salt
- Freshly ground black pepper.
- 1 yellow summer squash, grated
- 1/3 cups of carrot, grated
- a third cup bread crumbs
- 2 tablespoons olive oil

Method:

1. In a medium mixing bowl, combine the cream cheese, egg, oregano, salt, and pepper. Mix in the squash and carrots well. Add the bread crumbs and mix well.
2. Form roughly 2 teaspoons of this mixture into a 1/2-inch thick patty. Rep with the remaining mixture. Olive oil should be brushed on the fritters.
3. Air-fry for 7 to 9 minutes, or until crisp and golden.

Cooking hint:

Because yellow summer squash has a thin skin, there is no need to peel it before cooking. If you wish to use zucchini in this recipe, peel it first since the skin is harder than the flesh.

Cost per serving:

234 calories; 17 grams total fat; 6 grams saturated fat; 64 milligrams cholesterol; 261 milligrams sodium, 6g protein; 2g fiber; 16g carbohydrate

GNOCCHI PESTO

Preparation time: 5 minutes/Cooking time: 20 minutes/Serves 4

Preheat the oven to 390°F.

Vegetarian

Gnocchi may be purchased in the supermarket's pasta area in a shelf-stable packet that does not need refrigeration. Cooking them in an air fryer is different from boiling them; expect them to be crispy and tender.

Ingredients:

- 1 tablespoon of olive oil
- 1 onion, finely chopped
- 3 sliced garlic cloves
- 1 (16-ounce) package shelf-stable gnocchi
- 1 pesto jars (8 oz.)
- 1/3 cup grated Parmesan cheese

Method:

1. In a 6-by-6-by-2-inch pan, combine the oil, onion, garlic, and gnocchi, and place in the air fryer.
2. Bake for 10 minutes before removing the pan and stirring.
3. Return the pan to the air fryer and cook for an additional 8 to 13 minutes, or until the gnocchi are lightly browned and crisp.
4. Take the pan out of the air fryer. Serve right away with the pesto and Parmesan cheese.

What Did You Know? The word gnocchi is pronounced " nyuk-ee." They are 1-inch long oval dumplings with ridges on one side. They may be cooked in a variety of ways, including frying, baking, and boiling.

Cost per serving:

646 calories; 32 grams total fat; 7 grams saturated fat; 103 milligrams cholesterol; 461 milligrams sodium,2g fiber; 69g carbohydrate; 22g protein

TUNA SANDWICHES ON ENGLISH MUFFINS

Preparation time: 8 minutes/Cooking time: 5 minutes/Serves 4

Grill 390°F

FAST, FAMILY FAVORITE

Unless you want to eat dry cereal, there probably isn't a speedier recipe on the globe! A hefty sandwich made with toasted English muffins, melted cheese, and a chilled spicy tuna salad can be produced with only a few ingredients and 13 minutes.

Ingredients:

- 1 can (6 oz.) drained chunk light tuna
- 1 quart mayonnaise
- 2 tablespoons mustard
- 1 teaspoon fresh lemon juice
- Two minced green onions.
- 3 English muffins, slashed with a fork.
- 3 tbsp of softened butter.
- 6 slices of provolone or Muenster cheese thinly sliced.

Method:

1. Combine the tuna, mayonnaise, mustard, lemon juice, and green onions in a small mixing bowl.
2. The sliced side of the English muffins should be brushed with butter. In the air fryer, cook the butter side up for 2 to 4 minutes, or until light golden brown. Take the muffins out of the air fryer basket.
3. Return the muffins to the air fryer and top them with one piece of cheese.
4. Grill the cheese for 2 to 4 minutes, or until it melts and begins to color.
5. Remove the muffins from the oven and top them with the tuna mixture before serving.

Suggestions for an ingredient:

Choose pole-caught tuna if you're worried about sustainability.

Cost per serving:

389 calories; 23 grams total fat; 10 grams saturated fat; 50 milligrams cholesterol; 495 milligrams sodium, 25g of carbohydrates, 3g of fiber, and 21g of protein

MELTS WITH TUNA AND ZUCCHINI

Preparation time: 15 minutes/Cooking time: 10 minutes/Serves 4

Preheat the grill to 340°F.

Gluten-Free

A tuna melt is a typical dinner dish that is frequently grilled with butter. The air fryer produces a delicious melted sandwich with the minimum amount of additional fat. Zoodles add color, taste, and nutrition to this take on a classic.

Ingredients:

- Four corn tortillas.
- 3 tbsp of softened butter.
- 1 can (6 oz.) drained chunk light tuna
- 1 cup shredded zucchini, patted dry with a kitchen towel
- 1/3 cups of mayonnaise
- 2 tablespoons mustard
- 1 cup shredded Cheddar or Colby cheese

Method:

1. Spread the softened butter on the tortillas. Place the tortillas in the air fryer basket and cook for 2 to 3 minutes, or until crisp. After removing from the basket, set aside.
2. In a medium mixing dish, combine the tuna, zucchini, mayonnaise, and mustard.
3. Distribute the tuna mixture evenly among the toasted tortillas. Top each with some of the shredded cheese.
4. Grill for 2 to 4 minutes in the air fryer, or until the tuna mixture is hot and the cheese melts and begins to brown. Serve

Suggestions for an ingredient:

Most supermarket shops sell canned tuna in either water or oil. Although oil-canned tuna has a greater taste, water-canned tuna has fewer calories. For the finest taste and texture, use chunk light tuna.

Cost per serving:

428 calories; 30 grams total fat; 13 grams saturated fat; 71 milligrams cholesterol; 410 milligrams sodium, 19g of carbohydrates; 3g of fiber; 22g of protein

SANDWICHES WITH GRILLED CHEESE AND SHRIMP

Preparation time: 10 minutes/Cooking time: 5 minutes/Serves 4

Preheat the grill to 400°F.

FAST

The air fryer allows you to prepare grilled cheese sandwiches without having to flip them or linger over the stove watching them. In this simple recipe, you can use your favorite cheese.

Ingredients:

- 1 ¼ pound of shredded Colby, Cheddar, or Havarti cheese.
- 1 can (6 oz.) drained small shrimp
- 3 tablespoons mayonnaise
- 2 tbsp. minced green onion.
- 4 slices of whole-wheat or whole-grain bread
- 2 tablespoons softened butter

Method:

1. In a medium mixing bowl, add the cheese, shrimp, mayonnaise, and green onion.
2. This mixture should be spread over two pieces of bread. Top each sandwich with the remaining pieces of bread to create two sandwiches. Spread the sandwiches with a thin layer of butter.
3. Grill for 5 to 7 minutes in the air fryer or until the bread is golden and crisp and the cheese is melted. Serve it warm, cut in half.

A suggestion for a substitution:

Try substituting canned crabmeat, chicken, or tuna for the shrimp in this dish. For a vegetarian option, omit the shrimp and substitute 1 cup of a different variety of cheese.

Cost per serving:

276 calories; 14 grams total fat; 6 grams saturated fat; 115 milligrams cholesterol; 573 milligrams sodium , 22g protein; 2g fiber; 16g carbohydrate

SHRIMP CROQUETTES

Preparation time: 12 minutes/Cooking time: 8 minutes/Serves 3 to 4

390°F FRYING

Family member's favorite:

Croquettes are produced by combining finely minced meat with bread crumbs and eggs, then shaping them into little balls or patties and deep-frying them. You can prepare a guilt-free version of this delectable meal using an air fryer.

Ingredients:

- 2/3 pound cooked shelled and deveined shrimp
- 1 1/2 cups of bread crumbs (divided)
- 1 egg, beaten
- 2 tablespoons lemon juice
- two green onions, finely chopped
- 1/2 tsp. dried basil
- A pinch of salt
- Freshly ground black pepper.
- 2 tablespoons olive oil

Method:

1. Chop the shrimp finely. Take approximately 1 tablespoon of the finely chopped shrimp and mince it until it resembles a paste. Place aside.
2. Combine 1/2 cups of the bread crumbs, the egg, and the lemon juice in a medium mixing basin. Allow for a 5-minute resting period.
3. In a mixing bowl, combine the bread crumbs, shrimp, green onions, basil, salt, and pepper.
4. In a shallow dish, combine the remaining 1 cup bread crumbs with the olive oil; mix thoroughly.
5. Form the shrimp mixture into 1 1/2-inch round balls with your palms and press firmly. Coat the bread crumb mixture on top.
6. Cook the little croquettes in batches for 6 to 8 minutes, or until golden and crisp. Serve with cocktail sauce for dipping if desired.
7. Suggestions for an ingredient
8. Make a small incision along the back of each shrimp to reveal the black vein. Remove it with the point of a knife or by washing it under cold running water.

330 calories; 12 grams total fat; 2 grams saturated fat; 201 milligrams cholesterol; 539 milligrams sodium, 24g protein; 2g fiber; 31g carbohydrate

SHRIMP SALSA ON A DUTCH PANCAKE

Preparation time: 5 minutes/Cooking time: 10 minutes/Serves 4

Preheat the oven to 390°F.

FAST

It is not necessary for a Dutch pancake to be sweet! This savory version is filling for lunch, particularly when topped with a spicy salsa combination and delicate shrimp. The secret to mastering this meal is to go rapidly through the first few recipe stages.

Ingredients:

- 1 tbsp plus 2 tbsp butter
- three eggs
- 1/2 cups of all-purpose flour
- ½ gallon of milk
- 1/8 teaspoons of salt
- 1 gallon salsa
- 1 cup thawed completely cooked frozen tiny shrimp

Method:

1. Preheat the air fryer basket with a 6-by-6-by-2-inch pan in it. Heat the butter in a small saucepan until it melts.
2. In a medium bowl, quickly add the eggs, flour, milk, and salt. Beat vigorously with an eggbeater until the mixture is well-mixed and frothy, and then stir in the sugar.
3. Remove the basket and pan from the air fryer with care, tilting the pan so the butter coats the bottom. Pour the batter into the heated pan and return it to the fryer.
4. 12 to 16 minutes or until the pancake is puffy and golden brown.
5. Combine the salsa and shrimp in a mixing bowl and serve on top of the pancake.
6. Cooking tip: Thawing frozen fully cooked shrimp is simple. Simply place the shrimp in a colander and run cold water over them for a few minutes. Drain the shrimp and pat them dry before using.

Cost per serving:

213 calories; 9 grams of total fat; 5 grams of saturated fat; 198 milligrams of cholesterol; 593 milligrams of sodium, 14g protein; 2g fiber; 18g carbohydrate

SCALLOPS WITH DILL STEAM

Time To Prepare: 5 Minutes/Time To Cook: 4 Minutes/Serves 4

STEAM 390°F

<u>FAST</u>

This dish is perfect for an elegant — but quick — lunch. Alternatively, increase the quantity of scallops and serve them for supper. As the scallops cook, they expel liquid, which enters the pan under the basket and steams the fish. Serve with toast points or rice as a side dish.

Ingredients:

- One pound of sea scallops
- 1 teaspoon fresh lemon juice
- 2 tbsp extra-virgin olive oil
- 1 teaspoon dried dill
- A pinch of salt
- Freshly ground black pepper.

<u>Method:</u>

1. Look for a little muscle linked to the side of the scallops and peel it off and discard it.
2. Combine the scallops, lemon juice, olive oil, dill, salt, and pepper in a mixing bowl.
3. Place the air fryer basket in the air fryer.
4. Steam for 4 to 5 minutes, flipping the basket once while cooking, or until the scallops are firm when tested with a finger. The interior temperature should be at least 145°F.

Suggestions for an ingredient:

Scallops are classified into two types: bay scallops and sea scallops. They're both rather varied in size, with one being quite small and the other quite enormous.

Here's a simple method for remembering which is which: Because a bay is smaller than the sea, bay scallops are smaller.

<u>Cost per serving:</u>

121 calories; 3 grams total fat; 0 grams saturated fat; 37 milligrams cholesterol; 223 milligrams sodium, 19g protein; 3g carbohydrate; 0g fiber

SANDWICHES WITH CHICKEN PITA.

Preparation time: 10 minutes/Cooking time: 10 minutes/Serves 4

Preheat the oven to 380°F.

Family member's favorite:

Pita bread is great for sandwiches, but if you've just used cold ingredients in these small pockets, you're in for a surprise. Chicken, onion, and bell peppers are cooked until soft before being stuffed into pitas with fresh vegetables and vinaigrette.

Ingredients:

- 2 boneless, skinless chicken breasts (1-inch cubes)
- 1 tsp red onion, chopped
- 1 red bell pepper, sliced
- 1/3 cups of Italian salad dressing (distributed)
- 1/2 tsp. dried thyme
- 4 pita pockets, divided
- 2 cups butter lettuce, shredded
- 1 cup chopped cherry tomatoes

Method:

1. In the air fryer basket, combine the chicken, onion, and bell pepper. Toss with 1 tablespoon of the Italian salad dressing and the herbs.
2. Bake for 9–11 minutes, or until the chicken reaches 165°F on a food thermometer, tossing once.
3. Toss the chicken and veggies with the remaining salad dressing in a mixing bowl.
4. Assemble the sandwiches by layering pita pockets, butter lettuce, and cherry tomatoes.

A suggestion for a substitution:

This simple dish may be prepared with either cubed pork tenderloin or cubed chicken thighs. Both of these meats will cook for a few minutes longer than the chicken breasts. Cook the pork until it reaches 145° F and the chicken thighs until they reach 165° F.

Cost per serving:

414 calories; 19 grams total fat; 4 grams saturated fat; 101 milligrams cholesterol; 253 milligrams sodium, 2 g fiber; 22 g carbohydrate; 36 g protein

KING'S CHICKEN

Preparation time: 10 minutes/Cooking time: 17 minutes/Serves 4

Preheat the oven to 350°F.

Family member's favorite:

Chicken à la King is another evening staple, although it may also be eaten during lunch. Tender chicken is cooked in a white sauce before being served on crusty bread.

Ingredients:

- 2 boneless, skinless chicken breasts (1-inch cubes)
- 8 button mushrooms, sliced
- 1 red bell pepper, chopped
- 1 tablespoon of olive oil
- 1 box refrigerated Alfredo sauce (10 oz.)
- 1/2 tsp. dried thyme
- Six slices of French bread
- 2 tablespoons softened butter

Method:

1. In the air fryer basket, combine the chicken, mushrooms, and bell pepper.
2. Drizzle the olive oil over the salad and toss to coat.
3. Cook for 10 to 15 minutes, or until the chicken registers 165°F on a food thermometer, tossing once throughout the cooking time.
4. Transfer the chicken and veggies to a 6-inch metal mixing bowl and toss with the Alfredo sauce and thyme. Return to the air fryer for another 3–4 minutes, or until heated through.
5. Meanwhile, put the butter on the French bread pieces. When the chicken is done, remove the pan from the basket and place the bread, butter-side up, in the basket. Toast for 2–4 minutes, or until golden brown.
6. Arrange the bread on a platter and top with the chicken.

A Tip for the Air Fryer:

If your air fryer did not come with a pan for cooking items in the basket, get one! Many kitchen supply businesses sell 6-by-6-by-2-inch pans. In addition, a 6-inch metal bowl may contain components and mixes that are too big for the pan. Just make sure the bowl fits inside the basket of your air fryer.

Cost per serving:

744 calories; 32 grams total fat; 15 grams saturated fat; 142 milligrams cholesterol; 3,904 milligrams sodium; 64 grams carbohydrates; 2 grams fiber; 50 grams protein

SANDWICHES WITH SWEET AND SPICY BACON AND BELL PEPPERS

Preparation time: 15 minutes/Cooking time: 7 minutes/Serves 4

Preheat the grill to 350°F.

Family member's favorite:

Precooked bacon, which can be found in the meat area of the store, is an excellent convenience dish that works well in the air fryer. It simply needs to be heated since it is fully cooked. It also produces much less fat than raw bacon, so the air fryer will not smoke.

Ingredients:

- 1/3-cup hot barbecue sauce
- 2 tablespoons honey
- 8 precooked bacon pieces, divided into thirds
- 1 red bell pepper, sliced
- 1 yellow bell pepper, sliced
- 3 halved pita pockets
- 1 1/4 cups of shredded butter lettuce
- two thinly sliced tomatoes

Method:

1. Combine the barbecue sauce and honey in a small bowl. Brush the bacon pieces, as well as the red and yellow pepper slices, gently with this mixture.
2. Grill the peppers in the air fryer basket for 4 minutes. Shake the basket again, then add the bacon and cook for 2 minutes, or until the bacon is browned and the peppers are soft.
3. Fill the pita halves with the bacon, peppers, any leftover barbecue sauce, lettuce, and tomatoes and serve right away.

A suggestion for a substitution:

You may substitute Canadian bacon for the precooked bacon. Cook each slice of Canadian bacon into three pieces according to the instructions.

Cost per serving:

358 calories; 17 grams total fat; 5 grams saturated fat; 42 milligrams cholesterol; 1,228 milligrams sodium, 35g of carbohydrates, 3g of fiber, and 17g of protein

APPETIZERS

POT STICKERS STEAMED

Preparation time: 20 minutes; cooking time: 10 minutes; yield: 30 pot stickers

STEAM AT 360 DEGREES F

A Vegetarian Family Favorite:

Pot stickers are little Chinese dumplings that may be filled with anything you desire, but they're usually filled with meat or vegetables. Look for wonton wrappers in the vegetable area of your grocery store to prepare these vegetarian appetizers.

Ingredients:

- 1/2 cups of finely diced cabbage
- 1/4 cups of red bell pepper, finely chopped
- two green onions, finely chopped
- 1 egg, beaten
- 2 tablespoons cocktail sauce
- 2 tsp (low sodium) soy sauce
- 30 wrappings for wontons
- 3 tbsp water plus a little extra for brushing the wrappers

Method:

1. Combine the cabbage, pepper, green onions, egg, cocktail sauce, and soy sauce in a small mixing bowl.
2. One spoonful of the mixture should be placed in the middle of each wonton wrapper. Fold the wrapper in half, covering the filling; wet the sides and seal. You may crimp the wrapper's edges with your fingers to make them seem like pot stickers from restaurants. Water should be brushed over them.
3. In the pan under the air fryer basket, add 3 tablespoons of water. Cook the pot stickers in two batches for 9 to 10 minutes, or until hot and lightly browned on the bottoms.

A suggestion for a substitution:

Other veggies that may be used in this dish are maize, baby peas, and diced zucchini or summer squash. You might also add finely chopped leftover cooked meat, such as pork or chicken.

Size of serving (3 pot stickers):

291 calories, 2g total fat, 0g saturated fat, 35mg cholesterol, 649mg sodium, 57g carbohydrate, 3g fiber, and 10g protein

SKEWERS OF BEEF AND MANGO

Preparation time: 10 minutes/Cooking time: 5 minutes/Serves 4

Grill 390°F

Quick and gluten-free:

In the air fryer, any kabob or skewered dish cooks nicely. The meat becomes tender with a tiny crust while the fruit caramelizes and softens.

Ingredients:

- 3/4-pound beef sirloin tip, diced into 1-inch chunks.
- 2 tablespoons balsamic vinaigrette
- 1 tablespoon of olive oil
- 1 tablespoon honey
- 1/2 tsp. dried marjoram
- A pinch of salt
- Freshly ground black pepper.
- A single mango?

Method:

1. In a medium mixing bowl, combine the beef cubes, balsamic vinegar, olive oil, honey, marjoram, salt, and pepper. Mix thoroughly, and then use your hands to massage the marinade into the steak. Place aside.
2. To prepare the mango, lay it on its side and remove the peel with a sharp knife. Then, using a sharp knife, gently cut around the circular depression to remove the flesh. Make 1-inch cubes out of the mango.
3. Thread metal skewers with three meat cubes and two mango cubes alternately.
4. In the air fryer basket, grill the skewers for 4 to 7 minutes, or until the meat is browned and at least 145°F.

A suggestion for a substitution:

If you can't locate a ripe mango, you may substitute peaches or nectarines for it in this recipe. Any mature stone fruit will yield slightly and smell pleasant when gently squeezed.

Cost per serving:

242 calories; 9 grams total fat; 3 grams saturated fat; 76 milligrams cholesterol; 96 milligrams sodium, 1g fiber; 13g carbohydrate; 26g protein

FRIES WITH CURRIED SWEET POTATOES

Preparation time: 5 minutes/Cooking time: 8 to 12 minutes/Serves 4

Preheat the oven to 390°F.

FAMILY FAVORITE, GLUTEN-FREE:

If you've never had sweet potato fries before, they could just become your new favorite!

The potatoes are crisp and delicate, and when coated in butter and curry spice, they take on an appealing taste, particularly when paired with this creamy dip.

Ingredients:

- 1 quart soured cream
- 1/2 pound mango chutney
- 3 tablespoons curry powder (divided)
- 4 cups of sweet potato fries, frozen
- 1 tablespoon of olive oil
- A pinch of salt
- Freshly ground black pepper.

Method:

1. In a small mixing dish, combine the sour cream, chutney, and 1 1/2 tablespoons of curry powder. After thoroughly mixing, set aside.
2. In a medium mixing basin, combine the sweet potatoes. Drizzle with olive oil and season with the remaining 1 1/2 tablespoons of curry powder, salt, and pepper to taste.
3. Place the potatoes in the basket of the air fryer. Cook for 8 to 12 minutes, or until the basket is crisp, hot, and golden brown, shaking once throughout the cooking time.
4. Serve the fries with the chutney dip in a serving basket.

A suggestion for a substitution:

Fresh sweet potatoes may be substituted with the frozen precut fries. Use a sharp knife or mandoline to cut one or two sweet potatoes into 1/3-inch-thick strips. Use as indicated in the recipe, but extend the cooking time.

Cost per serving:

323 calories; 10 grams total fat; 4 grams saturated fat; 13 milligrams cholesterol; 138 milligrams sodium, Carbohydrates (58 g), Fiber (7 g), and Protein (3 g)

YOGURT-SPICED KALE CHIPS SAUCE

Preparation time: 10 minutes/Cooking time: 5 minutes/Serves 4

390°F FRYING

FAMILY FAVORITE, VEGETARIAN AND GLUTEN-FREE:

Kale chips are unique, tasty, and very healthy. Despite its high water content, this strong leafy green fries very nicely. The spicy dipping sauce complements the crisp chips well.

Ingredients:

- 1 cup unsweetened Greek yogurt
- 3 tbsp lemon juice
- 2 tablespoons honey mustard
- 1/2 tsp. dried oregano
- one pound curly kale
- 2 tablespoons olive oil
- 1/2 teaspoons of salt
- 1/8 teaspoon ground black pepper

Method:

1. Set aside the yogurt, lemon juice, honey mustard, and oregano in a small dish.
2. With a sharp knife, remove the stems and ribs from the kale. Leaves should be cut into 2- to 3-inch chunks.
3. Toss the kale in a bowl with the olive oil, salt, and pepper. With your hands, massage the oil into the leaves.
4. Cook the kale in batches for around 5 minutes, shaking the basket once while cooking. Serve with the yogurt sauce on the side.

Suggestions for an ingredient:

Kale comes in a variety of colors and shapes. Tuscan kale (also known as dinosaur kale or lacinato) is the toughest and creates the best chips. Curly kale, the most common form seen in supermarkets, may get a little frizzy when cooked in the air fryer, but it is still excellent.

Cost per serving:

154 calories; 8 grams of total fat; 2 grams of saturated fat; 3 milligrams of cholesterol; 378 milligrams of sodium,8g protein; 1g fiber; 13g carbohydrate

TRIANGLES OF PHYLLO ARTICHOKE

Preparation time: 15 minutes; cooking time: 9 minutes; yields 18 triangles.

Preheat the oven to 400°F.

Vegetarian:

Wrapped in crisp phyllo pastry, a creamy filling is cooked till golden and crispy. This classic will be a hit with your guests. If you want to up the spiciness, use marinated artichoke hearts in this recipe.

Ingredients:

- Ricotta cheese (1/4 c)
- 1 egg white, beaten
- 1/3 cups of drained minced artichoke hearts
- 3 tablespoons shredded mozzarella
- 1/2 tsp. dried thyme
- 6 thawed frozen phyllo dough sheets
- 2 tbsp. softened butter.

Method:

1. In a small mixing dish, combine the ricotta cheese, egg white, artichoke hearts, mozzarella cheese, and thyme.
2. While working, keep the phyllo dough moistened with a wet dish towel. Place one sheet on the work area at a time and cut it into thirds lengthwise.
3. Place approximately 1 1/2 teaspoons of the filling at the base of each strip. Fold the bottom right-hand tip of the phyllo over the filling in a triangle, and then continue folding into a triangle. To seal the edges, brush each triangle with butter. Repeat with the rest of the phyllo dough and filling.

4. Bake for 3 to 4 minutes, 6 at a time, or until the phyllo is golden brown and crisp.

A suggestion for a substitution:

In lieu of the artichoke hearts, you may use whatever you like in this filling. Try spinach, cooked shrimp, or cooked sausage, or make it vegetarian by using just grated cheese.

Per serving = 3 triangles

271 calories, 17g total fat, 7g saturated fat, 19mg cholesterol, 232mg sodium, 23g carbohydrate, 5g fiber, and 9g protein.

SPINACH DIP WITH CARAMELIZED BREAD KNOTS

Preparation time: 12 minutes/Cooking time: 16 to 21 minutes/Serves 6

Preheat the oven to 320°F.

Vegetarian:

This delicious appetizer has creamy hot spinach dip topped with breadstick dough knots. Place the pan on a trivet to serve so your guests can peel off the bread knots and sop up the dip! Cooking spray that is nonstick

Ingredients:

- 1 (8-ounce) box cubed cream cheese
- 1/4-cup soured cream
- 1/2 cups of thawed and drained frozen chopped spinach
- 1/2 cups of shredded Swiss cheese
- 2 green onions, chopped
- 1/2 refrigerated breadstick dough (11 oz.)
- 2 TBSP. Softened butter
- 3 tbsp grated Parmesan cheese

Method:

1. Use nonstick cooking spray on a 6-by-6-by-2-inch baking pan.
2. Mix together the cream cheese, sour cream, spinach, Swiss cheese, and green onions in a medium mixing basin. Bake for 8 minutes, or until heated through in the prepared pan.
3. While the dip bakes, unroll six of the breadsticks and cut them in half crosswise to produce 12 pieces.
4. Stretch each piece of dough gently and tie it into a loose knot; tuck the ends in.

5. Remove the dip from the air fryer when it is hot and gently arrange each bread knot on top of the dip, covering the whole surface. Brush each knot with melted butter and top with Parmesan cheese.
6. Bake the bread knots for 8 to 13 minutes or until golden brown and cooked through.

Suggestions for an ingredient:

After you've finished the dip and eaten it, wrap the leftover breadstick dough pieces in butter and cheese and bake them in the air fryer at 300 °F for approximately half the time advised on the container. Serve with soup or freeze it for later use.

Cost per serving: 264 calories; 23 grams of total fat; 14 grams of saturated fat; 68 milligrams of cholesterol; 270 milligrams of sodium, 8g protein; 7g carbohydrate; 0g fiber

ARANCINI

Preparation time: 15 minutes/Cooking time: 16 to 22 minutes/Makes 16 Arancin

Preheat the oven to 400°F.

A Vegetarian Family Favorite:

Arancini are little rice balls that are deep-fried and occasionally loaded with cheese or other savory fillings. They are popular in Italy. This dish may be made using leftover risotto or with leftover rice from a Chinese restaurant.

Ingredients:

- 2 cups cooked and cooled leftover rice or risotto
- Two beaten eggs
- 1 1/2 cup bread crumbs (split panko)
- 1/2 cups of Parmesan cheese, grated
- 2 tbsp of fresh basil, minced
- melted mozzarella cheese cubes measuring 16" x 3/4"
- 2 tablespoons olive oil

Method:

1. Combine the rice, eggs, 1/2 cups of bread crumbs, Parmesan cheese, and basil in a medium mixing basin. Make 16 1 1/2-inch balls out of this mixture.
2. Make a hole with your finger in each of the balls and insert a mozzarella cube. Wrap the cheese in the rice mixture tightly.

3. In a small dish, mix the remaining 1 cup bread crumbs with the olive oil. Coat the rice balls with the bread crumbs.
4. Arancini should be cooked in batches for 8 to 11 minutes, or until golden brown.

What Did You Know? Arancini, also known as suppl or rice frittata in Italy, are served on the street as a snack dish. They are significantly larger in that country. They are around the size of an orange and are often shaped into a cone shape.

2 Arancini = 2 servings

378 calories; 11g total fat; 4g saturated fat; 361mg sodium; 53g carbohydrate; 2g fiber; 16g protein

BRUSCHETTA WITH PESTO

Time To Prepare: 10 Minutes/Time To Cook: 4 to 8 Minutes/Serves 4

Bake at 350°F.

Fast and vegetarian:

Pesto is a traditional Italian sauce prepared with fresh basil, olive oil, garlic, and Parmesan cheese. In this recipe, the vibrant and powerful sauce is combined with fresh tomatoes and smeared over warm, crunchy cheese toast.

Ingredients:

- 8 slices of 12" thick French bread
- 2 tablespoons softened butter
- 1 cup shredded mozzarella cheese
- 1/2 cup basil pesto
- 1 cup chopped grape tomatoes
- 2 green onions, finely sliced

Method:

1. Spread the butter on the bread and set it butter-side up in the air fryer basket. Bake the bread for 3 to 5 minutes, or until it is light golden brown.
2. Remove the bread from the basket and sprinkle some of the cheese on top of each slice. Return the basket to the oven in stages and bake until the cheese melts, 1 to 3 minutes.
3. Meanwhile, in a separate bowl, mix the pesto, tomatoes, and green onions.

4. Remove the bread from the air fryer and set it on a serving platter after the cheese has melted. Serve with a dollop of pesto on top of each piece.

Suggestions for an ingredient:

If you go to the store, you can find basil pesto and other types of pesto, such as a sauce made from sun-dried tomatoes.

Cost per serving:

462 calories; 25 grams total fat; 10 grams saturated fat; 38 milligrams cholesterol; 822 milligrams sodium, Carbohydrates (41g), Fiber (3g), and Protein (19g)

TORTELLINI IN A SPICY SAUCE WITH FRIED TORTELLINI SAUCE

Preparation time: 8 minutes/Cooking time: 20 minutes/Serves 4

Temperature of the fryer: 380 °F

A Vegetarian Family Favorite:

Did you know you could fry tortellini to make a gourmet appetizer? Frozen tortellini may be found in the freezer department of most supermarkets. Serve with a hot tomato sauce on the side for dipping.

Ingredients:

- one-quarter cup mayonnaise
- 2 tablespoons mustard
- One egg
- 1/2 cups of all-purpose flour
- 1/2 tsp. dried oregano
- 1 ½ cup bread crumbs
- 2 tablespoons olive oil
- 2 cups of frozen tortellini with cheese

Method:

1. In a small mixing dish, combine the mayonnaise and mustard.
2. Place aside.
3. Beat the egg in a small basin. Combine the flour and oregano in a separate basin. Mix up the bread crumbs and olive oil in a separate bowl.
4. To coat, dip a few tortellini at a time into the egg, then into the flour, then back into the egg, and lastly into the bread crumbs. Cooking in batches in the air fryer basket.

5. Cook for 10 minutes, shaking halfway through, or until the tortellini are crisp and golden brown on the exterior. Serve with mayonnaise.

A suggestion for a substitution:

This method may also be used to make ravioli or pierogies, which are huge Eastern European dumplings. The ravioli will take around 15 minutes to cook, and the pierogies will take about 20 minutes to cook until heated through.

Cost per serving:

698 calories; 31 grams total fat; 4 grams saturated fat; 66 milligrams cholesterol; 832 milligrams sodium, Carbohydrates (88g), Fiber (3g), and Protein (18g)

TOAST TOPPED WITH SHRIMP

Preparation time: 15 minutes; cooking time: 6 to 12 minutes; yields 12 toasts.

Preheat the oven to 350°F.

Family member's favorite:

Shrimp toast is a popular appetizer in Chinese restaurants. Traditionally, chopped shrimp are combined with egg whites and spices and placed over toast before being deep-fried till crisp. Because you don't have to deal with heated oil or flip the small toasts as they cook, the air fryer makes this dish a snap.

Ingredients:

- 3 firm slices of white bread
- 2/3 cup raw shrimp, peeled and deveined, coarsely chopped
- 1 egg white, beaten
- 2 minced garlic cloves.
- 2 tablespoons cornstarch
- 1/4 teaspoon powdered ginger
- A pinch of salt
- Freshly ground black pepper.
- 2 tablespoons olive oil

Method:

1. Using a sharp knife, remove the crusts off the bread; crush the crusts to form bread crumbs. Place aside.
2. Mix the shrimp, egg white, garlic, cornstarch, ginger, salt, and pepper in a small bowl.

3. Spread the shrimp mixture evenly on the bread, all the way to the edges. Cut each slice into four strips using a sharp knife.
4. Pat the bread crumbs and olive oil mixture onto the shrimp mixture. Place the shrimp toasts in a single layer in the air fryer basket; you may need to cook in batches.
5. Cook for 3–6 minutes, or until crispy and golden brown.

A suggestion for a substitution:

Replace the shrimp in this recipe with finely chopped cooked crabmeat, or use ground chicken or ground turkey instead.

1 serving = 2 toasts: 7g carbohydrate; 0g fiber; 9g protein; 121 calories; 6g total fat; 1g saturated fat; 72mg cholesterol; 158mg sodium; 7g carbohydrate; 0g fiber; 9g protein

TATER TOTS WITH BACON

Preparation time: 5 minutes/Cooking time: 17 minutes/Serves 4

Preheat the oven to 400°F.

FAVORITE OF THE GLUTEN-FREE FAMILY:

This dish is ideal for tailgating before the big game! The greatest comfort dish is the mix of potatoes, bacon, and cheese.

Ingredients:

- 24 tater tots (frozen)
- Six precooked bacon slices.
- 2 tablespoons maple syrup
- 1 cup shredded Cheddar cheese

Method:

1. In the air fryer basket, place the tater tots. Shake the basket midway during the frying time and air-fry for 10 minutes.
2. Meanwhile, shred the cheese and chop the bacon into 1-inch pieces.
3. Remove the potato tots from the air fryer basket and place them in a 6-by-6-by2-inch baking dish. Drizzle with maple syrup and sprinkle with bacon. Minutes in the air fryer or until the tots and bacon are crisp.
4. Place the cheese on top and air-fry for 2 minutes, or until the cheese is melted.

Suggestions for an ingredient:

For this dish, you can only use precooked bacon that does not need to be refrigerated. If you use ordinary bacon, it will give off too much fat, making the tater tots mushy rather than crisp.

Cost per serving:

374 calories; 22 grams total fat; 9 grams saturated fat; 40 milligrams cholesterol; 857 milligrams sodium, 13g protein; 34g carbohydrate; 2g fiber

BRUSCHETTA WITH HASH BROWNS

Preparation time: 7 minutes/Cooking time: 6 to 8 minutes/Serves 4

Preheat the oven to 400°F.

FAMILY FAVORITE, VEGETARIAN AND GLUTEN-FREE:

Bruschetta is an Italian dish that consists of crisp bread topped with toppings such as chopped tomatoes and herbs. Crisp hash brown patties replace bread in this dish. Frozen hash brown patties cook well in the air fryer, and they contain very little fat!

Ingredients:

- 4 thawed frozen hash brown patties.
- 1 tablespoon of olive oil
- 1/3 cup chopped cherry tomatoes
- 3 tbsp diced fresh mozzarella
- 2 tbsp grated Parmesan cheese
- 1 tablespoon balsamic vinegar
- 1 tbsp minced fresh basil

Method:

1. Place the hash brown patties in a single layer in the air fryer. Air-fry the potatoes for 6 to 8 minutes, or until crisp, hot, and golden brown.
2. Meanwhile, in a separate bowl, mix the olive oil, tomatoes, mozzarella, Parmesan, vinegar, and basil.
3. When the potatoes are cooked, gently take them from the basket and place them on a serving platter. Serve with the tomato mixture on top.

What Did You Know? Bruschetta is an Italian phrase that means "to roast over coals," and it refers to toasted bread. It comes in a variety of forms, including one in which the warm small toasts are simply rubbed with a sliced clove of fresh garlic.

Cost per serving:

6g total fat; 2g saturated fat; 6mg cholesterol; 81mg sodium; 14g carbohydrate; 2g fiber; 5g protein

POUTINE, WAFFLE FRY

Preparation time: 10 minutes/Cooking time: 15 to 17 minutes/Serves 4

Temperature of the fryer: 380 °F

Family member's favorite:

Poutine is a classic French Canadian dish that consists of fries covered with cheese curds and beef sauce. Cooking it in the air fryer, of course, helps to reduce the calories. Other nutritious additions include grated cheese, chicken gravy, and vegetables!

Ingredients:

- 2 cups frozen waffle sliced fries
- 2 tbsp extra-virgin olive oil
- 1 red bell pepper, chopped
- Two sliced green onions.
- 1 cup shredded Swiss cheese
- 1/2 cup chicken gravy (canned)

Method:

1. Place the waffle fries in the air fryer basket and toss with olive oil. Air fries the fries for 10 to 12 minutes, or until crisp and light brown.
2. Shake the basket halfway during the cooking time to brown.
3. Top the fries with the pepper, green onions, and cheese in a 6-by-6-by-2-inch pan. 3 minutes in the air fryer or until the veggies are crisp and tender.
4. Remove the air fryer pan from the oven and sprinkle the gravy over the fries.
5. 2 minutes in the air fryer or until the gravy is hot. Serve it right away.

A suggestion for a substitution:

This dish may also be made using standard frozen French fries, but it will take a few minutes longer to cook. In this delicious meal, use your favorite cheese.

Cost per serving:

347 calories; 19 grams total fat; 7 grams saturated fat; 26 milligrams cholesterol; 435 milligrams sodium, 12g protein; 4g fiber; 33g carbohydrate

CRISPY CUBES OF BEEF

Preparation time: 10 minutes/Cooking time: 12 to 16 minutes/Serves 4

Preheat the oven to 360°F.

Family member's favorite:

Beef cooks well in an air fryer. This novel technique of dipping the beef in a cheese sauce and coating it in bread crumbs results in a crunchy, tiny bite with soft and juicy insides.

Ingredients:

- 1 pound sirloin tip cut into 1-inch pieces
- 1 cup (from a 16-ounce jar) pasta cheese sauce
- 1 1/2 cup bread crumbs
- 2 tablespoons olive oil
- 1/2 tsp. dried marjoram

Method:

1. Toss the meat with the spaghetti sauce in a medium bowl to coat.
2. Combine the bread crumbs, oil, and marjoram in a small basin and stir well. To completely coat the meat cubes, drop them into the bread crumbs mixture one at a time.
3. Cook the beef in two batches for 6 to 8 minutes, shaking the basket once while cooking, until it reaches 145°F and the exterior is crisp and brown. Use toothpicks or little forks to serve.

Cooking hint:

With the leftover spaghetti sauce, you can make a quick lunch. Simply prepare a cup or two of pasta while the sauce heats up in a pot. Combine the ingredients and serve.

Cost per serving:

554 calories; 22 grams total fat; 8 grams saturated fat; 112 milligrams cholesterol; 1,832 milligrams sodium, 44g protein; 2g fiber; 43g carbohydrate

BUFFALO CHICKEN BITES

Preparation time: 10 minutes/Cooking time: 14 to 18 minutes/Serves 4

Preheat the oven to 350°F.

Family member's favorite

These small nibbles are bursting with flavor. The delicate chicken is encased in a spicy sauce before being topped with crunchy bread crumbs. A cold dipping sauce is the ideal complement.

Ingredients:

- 2/3 pound soured cream
- 1/4 cups of salad dressing (creamy blue cheese)
- 1/4 cups of blue cheese crumbles
- 1 celery stalk, finely sliced
- 1 pound chicken tenders, cut into thirds crosswise
- 3 tablespoons Buffalo chicken wing sauce
- 1 cup panko bread crumbs
- 2 tablespoons olive oil

Method:

1. Set aside the sour cream, salad dressing, blue cheese, and celery in a small dish.
2. Combine the chicken pieces and Buffalo wing sauce in a medium mixing bowl and toss to coat. Allow it to sit while you prepare the bread crumbs.
3. In a dish, combine the bread crumbs and olive oil.
4. Coat the chicken in the bread crumb mixture, pressing each piece down to ensure the crumbs adhere.
5. Cook the chicken in batches for 7 to 9 minutes, shaking the basket once, until it reaches 165°F and is golden brown. Serve with a side of blue cheese sauce.

What Did You Know? Buffalo chicken wings were created at the Anchor Bar in Buffalo, New York, when the proprietor wanted to serve a large number of appetizers quickly. They were an instant smash, and the flavor—a scorching hot sauce with chilled blue cheese—is now a classic.

Cost per serving:

467 calories; 23 grams total fat; 8 grams saturated fat; 119 milligrams cholesterol; 821 milligrams sodium, 1g fiber; 22g carbohydrate; 43g protein

CHICKEN WINGS WITH A SWEET AND SPICY FLAVOR

Preparation time: 5 minutes; cooking time: 25 minutes; yields 16 wings.

Preheat the oven to 390°F.

Family member's favorite:

Chicken wings are an excellent appetizer for a big game or while cooking outdoors. The air fryer crisps and tenderizes the wings, and the sweet and spicy sauce adds the right finishing touch.

Ingredients:

- 8 pieces of chicken wings
- 1 tablespoon of olive oil
- 1/3 cup sugar, granulated
- 2 tablespoons honey
- 1/3 cup apple cider vinegar
- 2 minced garlic cloves.
- 1/2 tsp. dried red pepper flakes
- 1/4 tsp of salt

Method:

1. Each chicken wing should be cut into three parts. You will have one big, one medium, and one small end. Save the little end for stock or discard it.
2. Toss the wings with the oil in a medium basin. Cook for 20 minutes in the air fryer basket, shaking the basket twice while frying.
3. Meanwhile, mix together the sugar, honey, vinegar, red pepper flakes, and salt in a small basin.
4. Remove the wings from the air fryer basket and place them in a 6-by-6-by-2-inch baking dish. Toss the wings in the sauce to coat.
5. Return the wings to the air fryer and cook for 5 minutes, or until glazed.

Suggestions for an ingredient:

In the meat area, you may sometimes find "chicken Drumettes." They're made from the meaty portion of a chicken wing. Use around 10 of these instead of the cut-up entire wings in this recipe.

Serving size (4 wings): 438 calories; 16g total fat; 4g saturated fat; 151mg cholesterol; 299mg sodium; 21g carb; 0g fiber; 49g protein

FISH AND SEAFOOD RECIPES

PAELLA IN A FLASH

Preparation time: 7 minutes/Cooking time: 13 to 17 minutes/Serves 4

Preheat the oven to 340°F.

Gluten-Free:

Paella is a one-dish Spanish cuisine comprised of rice, vegetables, and fish. It's a breeze to make in the air fryer with a few convenience items. Serve with a fruit salad and a glass of rosé wine.

Ingredients:

- 1 bag thawed frozen cooked rice (10 oz.)
- 1 jar (6 oz.) drained and diced artichoke hearts
- 1/4 cups of broth (vegetarian)
- 1/2 teaspoons of turmeric
- 1/2 tsp. dried thyme
- 1 cup tiny cooked frozen shrimp
- 1/2 cups of thawed frozen baby peas
- 1 tomato, diced

Ingredients:

1. In a 6-by-6-by-2-inch pan, stir together the rice, artichoke hearts, vegetable broth, turmeric, and thyme.
2. Bake for 8 to 9 minutes, or until the rice is heated through in the air fryer.
3. Remove the shrimp, peas, and tomato from the air fryer and toss gently.5–8 minutes, or until the shrimp and peas are heated through and the paella is boiling.

A suggestion for a substitution:

If you like strongly flavored foods, try this dish with marinated artichoke hearts. Make sure to sample the marinade first! Use the liquid from the jar of artichokes in lieu of the vegetable broth for even more flavor.

Cost per serving:

345 calories; 1 gram total fat; 0 gram saturated fat; 144 milligrams cholesterol; 491 milligrams sodium, Carbohydrates (66g), Fiber (4g), and Protein (18g)

CRAB RATATOUILLE (CRAB RATATOUILLE)

Preparation time: 15 minutes/Cooking time: 11 to 14 minutes/Serves 4

Preheat the oven to 400°F.

Gluten-Free:

Ratatouille is traditionally made by stewing various vegetables and fresh herbs; however, you can make it in a fraction of the time with an air fryer. It looks even more elegant when crab is added to this delicate mix, making it classier.

Ingredients:

- 1 1/2 cups of peeled and diced eggplant
- 1 onion, chopped
- 1 red bell pepper, chopped
- Two big sliced tomatoes
- 1 tablespoon of olive oil
- 1/2 tsp. dried thyme
- 1/2 tsp. dried basil
- A pinch of salt
- Freshly ground black pepper.
- 1 1/2 cups of cooked crabmeat, peeled

Method:

1. In a 6-inch metal bowl, combine the eggplant, onion, bell pepper, tomatoes, olive oil, thyme, and basil. Season with salt and pepper to taste.
2. After 9 minutes of roasting, take the bowl from the air fryer and mix.
3. Cook for 2 to 5 minutes, or until the ratatouille is bubbling and the veggies are soft. Serve it right away.
4. Crabmeat can be purchased in a can, or tubs of shelled crab can be found at many large supermarket seafood counters.

Cost per serving:

147 calories; 5 grams total fat; 1 gram saturated fat; 71 milligrams cholesterol; 244 milligrams sodium, 16g protein; 10g carbohydrate; 4g fiber

MARISCOS TACOS

Preparation time: 15 minutes/Cooking time: 9 to 12 minutes/Serves 4

Preheat the oven to 400°F.

Family member's favorite:

Seafood tacos are popular in California, where fresh seafood is harvested off the coast every day. This easy meal is rich in taste and texture, and it's ideal for a hot summer evening.

Ingredients:

1. 1 pound white fish fillets, such as snapper
2. 1 tablespoon of olive oil
3. 3 tbsp. lemon juice, divided
4. 1 1/2 cups of red cabbage, chopped
5. 1/2 cup of salsa
6. 1/3-cup soured cream
7. 6 soft flour tortillas
8. Two peeled and sliced avocados

Method:

1. Brush the fish with olive oil and season with 1 tablespoon of lemon juice. Place the fish in the air fryer basket and cook for 9 to 12 minutes, or until it flakes when checked with a fork.
2. Meanwhile, in a medium mixing bowl, combine the remaining 2 tablespoons of lemon juice, cabbage, salsa, and sour cream. When the fish is done, take it from the air fryer basket and cut it into big chunks.
3. Allow each person to create their own taco by mixing the fish, tortillas, cabbage mixture, and avocados.
4. In this dish, you may use scallops, shrimp, lobster tails, or a variety of seafood. In the air fryer, cook until done, and then assemble the tacos with the other ingredients.

Calories in one serving:

491 calories, 29 grams total fat, 8 grams saturated fat, 71 milligrams cholesterol, and 323 milligrams sodium, 31g protein; 29g carbohydrate; 10g fiber

HERBED, CRISPY SALMON

Preparation time: 5 minutes/Cooking time: 9 to 12 minutes/Serves 4

Preheat the oven to 320°F.

<u>FAST</u>

Healthy salmon is an excellent component for air frying. The crunchy crust in this recipe—a combination of potato chips and bread crumbs—perfectly contrasts with the soft and juicy fish.

<u>Ingredients:</u>

- 4 skinless salmon fillets (6 oz.)
- 3 tablespoons honey mustard
- 1/2 tsp. dried thyme
- 1/2 tsp. dried basil
- 1/4 cups of bread crumbs (panko)
- 1/3-Cup CRUMBLED POTATO CHIPPIES
- 2 tablespoons olive oil

<u>Method:</u>

- Place the salmon on a serving platter. Combine the mustard, thyme, and basil in a small dish and distribute it equally over the salmon.
- Mix the bread crumbs and potato chips in a separate small bowl. Drizzle in the olive oil and stir to blend.
- Place the salmon in the air fryer basket and press the bread crumb mixture gently but firmly onto the top of each fillet.
- Bake for 9 to 12 minutes, or until the salmon reaches a temperature of at least 145°F on a meat thermometer and the topping is golden and crisp.

<u>Suggestions for an ingredient:</u>

Panko bread crumbs are sharper and have a distinct feel than conventional bread crumbs. Most stores have them in the baking section. If you can't locate them, normal bread crumbs will suffice. However, the quantity should be reduced to 1/4 cups.

<u>Calories in one serving:</u>

373 calories; 21 grams of total fat; 3 grams of saturated fat; 75 milligrams of cholesterol; 218 milligrams of sodium; 13 grams of carbohydrates; 1 gram of fiber; 34 grams of protein

ASIAN TUNA STEAMED

Preparation time: 10 minutes/Cooking time: 8 to 10 minutes/Serves 4

STEAM 390°F

Family member's favorite:

Steaming tuna yields exquisite results. Lemongrass, soy sauce, sesame oil, rice wine vinegar, and fresh ginger are among the fragrant Asian ingredients used in this dish.

Ingredients:

- 4 tuna steaks, tiny
- 2 tbsp. of low-sodium soy sauce
- 2 tbsp. sesame oil.
- 2 tablespoons rice wine vinegar
- 1 teaspoon grated fresh ginger
- 1/8 teaspoon ground black pepper
- 1 lemongrass stalk, halved
- 3 tbsp lemon juice
- On a dish, arrange the tuna steaks.

Method:

1. In a small mixing bowl, add the soy sauce, sesame oil, rice wine vinegar, and ginger. Pour this mixture over the tuna and let it marinate for 10 minutes. Gently rub the soy sauce mixture into both sides of the tuna.
2. Season with salt to taste.
3. Place the lemongrass on top of the steaks in the air fryer basket. In the pan under the basket, combine the lemon juice and 1 tablespoon of water.
4. Steam the tuna for 8 to 10 minutes, or until it reaches a temperature of at least 145°F. Remove the lemongrass before serving the tuna.

A Tip for the Air Fryer:

When this dish is cooking, keep an eye on the liquid in the pan under the air fryer basket. As the tuna cooks, it will release liquid, and you don't want the pan to overflow.

Cost per serving:

292 calories; 14 grams total fat; 3 grams saturated fat; 44 milligrams cholesterol; 513 milligrams sodium, 1 gram of carbohydrate; 0 gram of fiber; 38 gram of protein

STIR-FRY WITH TUNA AND VEGGIES

Preparation time: 15 minutes/Cooking time: 7 to 12 minutes/Serves 4

STIR-FRY 380 °F

Family member's favorite

Stir-fry dishes in the air fryer are simple to prepare. You just do not need to stir them up too much! Simply remove the basket from the air fryer and stir to blend. With steamed rice, serve.

Ingredients:

- 1 tablespoon of olive oil
- 1 red bell pepper, chopped
- 1 cup peeled and cut into 2-inch pieces green beans
- 1 onion, sliced
- Two garlic cloves, sliced
- 2 tbsp. of low-sodium soy sauce
- 1 tablespoon honey
- 1/2 pound fresh tuna, cubed

Method:

1. Combine the olive oil, pepper, green beans, onion, and garlic in a 6-inch metal bowl.
2. Cook for 4 to 6 minutes, stirring once, until crisp and tender in the air fryer. Stir in the soy sauce, honey, and tuna.
3. Cook for 3 to 6 minutes more, stirring once, until the tuna is cooked to your liking. Tuna may be served rare, medium-rare, or cooked till done.

A suggestion for a substitution:

In this simple dish, you may use whatever vegetable you like. Use roughly half a bag of frozen stir-fry veggies to make it even simpler. Alternatively, use chopped or sliced zucchini or yellow summer squash instead of the red bell pepper or green beans.

Cost per serving:

187 calories; 8 grams of total fat; 2 grams of saturated fat; 18 milligrams of cholesterol; 333 milligrams of sodium, 12 g of carbohydrates, 2 g of fiber, and 17 g of protein

Scallops with Spring Vegetables

Preparation time: 10 minutes/Cooking time: 7 to 10 minutes/Serves 4

Preheat the oven to 400°F.

Gluten-Free

Scallops cook quickly, making them great for a fast meal. When coupled with vivid green veggies, they create a beautiful supper. Scallops taste mild and sweet, even with little preparation.

Ingredients:

- 1/2 pound asparagus, cut into 2-inch sections after removing the ends
- 1 pound sugar snap peas
- One pound of sea scallops
- 1 teaspoon fresh lemon juice
- 2 tbsp extra-virgin olive oil
- 1/2 tsp. dried thyme
- A pinch of salt
- Freshly ground black pepper.

Method:

1. Fill the air fryer basket halfway with asparagus and sweet snap peas. Cook for 2 to 3 minutes, or until the veggies begin to soften.
2. Meanwhile, look for a little muscle linked to the side of the scallops and peel it off and discard it.
3. Toss the scallops with the lemon juice, olive oil, thyme, salt, and pepper in a medium bowl. Place it on top of the veggies in the air fryer basket.
4. Steam for 5 to 7 minutes, flipping the basket once during cooking, until the scallops are firm when touched with a finger and opaque in the middle, and the veggies are soft. Serve it right away.

A Tip for the Air Fryer:

If you have an air fryer with a divider, you can cook this dinner even quicker. Cook the scallops for 5 to 6 minutes on one side and the veggies for 5 to 6 minutes on the other.

Cost per serving:

162 calories; 4 grams total fat; 1 gram saturated fat; 37 milligrams cholesterol; 225 milligrams sodium, 10g of carbohydrates; 3g of fiber; 22g of protein

SNAPPER SCAMPI

Preparation time: 5 minutes/Cooking time: 8 to 10 minutes/Serves 4

Preheat the grill to 380°F.

Quick and gluten-free

The term "scampi" may refer to either giant shrimp or a meal that mixes shrimp with lemon, butter, and garlic. These items will be used to produce a simple meal using red snapper or arctic char fillets.

Ingredients:

- 4 skinless snapper or arctic char fillets (6 oz.)
- 1 tablespoon of olive oil
- 3 tbsp. lemon juice, divided
- 1/2 tsp. dried basil
- A pinch of salt
- Freshly ground black pepper.
- 2 tbsp. melted butter
- 2 minced garlic cloves.

Method:

1. Rub the fish fillets with 1 tablespoon each of lemon juice and olive oil.
2. Place it in the air fryer basket and season with basil, salt, and pepper.
3. Grill the salmon for 7 to 8 minutes, or until it flakes easily with a fork. Place the fish on a serving platter after removing it from the basket.
4. Cover up to stay warm.
5. In a 6-by-6-by-2-inch pan, combine the butter, remaining 2 tablespoons lemon juice, and garlic. Cook for 1 to 2 minutes in the air fryer, or until the garlic is sizzling. Pour this over the fish and serve.

What Did You Know? You can purchase bottled lemon and lime juice at the store, but for recipes like this one, when the taste is vital, squeeze the juice from a lemon just before you start cooking.

Cost per serving:

265 calories; 11 grams of total fat; 5 grams of saturated fat; 109 milligrams of cholesterol; 215 milligrams of sodium, 1 gram of carbohydrate; 0 gram of fiber; 39 gram of protein

SHRIMP IN COCONUT SAUCE

Preparation time: 15 minutes/Cooking time: 5 to 7 minutes/Serves 4

Preheat the oven to 400°F.

Family member's favorite

Tender shrimp covered in a bread crumb and coconut combination, air-fried to crisp perfection, and served with a pineapple dipping sauce sounds delectable. It's a great snack, but it can also serve as a main course when coupled with rice and a green salad.

Ingredients:

- 1 can (8 oz.) crushed pineapple
- 1 quart soured cream
- 1/4-cup pineapple chutney
- Two egg whites.
- 2/3 cup of cornstarch
- 2/3 cups of sugared coconut
- 1 cup panko bread crumbs
- 1 pound of uncooked big shrimp deveined and shelled if frozen.
- Misting with olive oil

Method:

1. Using a strainer, thoroughly drain the crushed pineapple, saving the juice.
2. In a small mixing bowl, combine the pineapple, sour cream, and preserves. Place aside.
3. In a small dish, whisk together 2 tablespoons of the reserved pineapple liquid and the egg whites. On a dish, spread out the cornstarch. In a separate dish, combine the coconut and bread crumbs.
4. Dip the shrimp in the cornstarch, shake off the excess, and then into the egg white mixture, followed by the coconut mixture.
5. Mist the shrimp with oil and place them in the air fryer basket. Air-fry the shrimp for 5 to 7 minutes, or until crisp and golden brown.

What Did You Know? The number of shrimp in a pound is used to rate them. Large shrimp are often priced at 26 to 30 cents per pound, while medium shrimp are priced at 36 to 45 cents per pound. They are available shelled, deveined, and ready to cook, as well as completely cooked.

Cost per serving:

524 calories; 14 grams of total fat; 9 grams of saturated fat; 251 milligrams of cholesterol; 251 milligrams of sodium,65g carbs; 4g fiber; 33g protein

FISH AND CHIPS

Time to Prepare: 10 Minutes/Time to Cook: 20 Minutes/Serves 4

Preheat the oven to 400°F.

FAVORITE OF THE GLUTEN-FREE FAMILY

In British slang, "chips" refers to French fries rather than potato chips. This traditional dish is simple to cook in an air fryer, particularly if it has a divider. Cook the potatoes first and keep them warm in a low oven while the fish cooks. Serve this dish with plenty of tartar sauce.

Ingredients:

- 4 fillets of fish (4 oz.)
- A pinch of salt
- Freshly ground black pepper.
- 1/2 tsp. dried thyme
- 1 egg white, beaten
- a quarter cup crushed potato chips
- 2 tbsp of olive oil (divided)
- 2 russet potatoes peeled and slashed.

Method:

1. Dry the fish fillets and season them with salt, pepper, and thyme. Place aside.
2. Beat the egg whites until frothy in a small basin. In a separate dish
3. Mix up the potato chips and 1 tablespoon of olive oil until well blended.
4. To coat, dip the fish fillets in the egg white, then in the crushed potato chip mixture.
5. Toss the remaining 1 tablespoon of olive oil with the fresh potato strips.
6. Divide the air fryer basket in half with your divider, then cook the chips and fish. The chips will take around 20 minutes to cook, and the fish will take about 10 to 12 minutes.

Suggestions for an ingredient:

Tartar sauce is made with 1/2 cup mayonnaise, 3 tablespoons chopped sweet pickles, 1 tablespoon lemon juice, and 1 tablespoon chopped fresh parsley.

Cost per serving:

374 calories; 16 grams total fat; 4 grams saturated fat; 62 milligrams cholesterol; 254 milligrams sodium, 30g protein; 4g fiber; 38g carbohydrate.

POULTRY RECIPES

Salad with Roasted Veggie Chicken

Preparation time: 10 minutes/Cooking time: 10 to 13 minutes/Serves 4

Preheat the oven to 400°F.

FAVORITE OF THE GLUTEN-FREE FAMILY

Have you had a warm chicken salad? It has a better taste than cold chicken salad and takes significantly less time to make. This one has a lot of vibrant elements.

Ingredients:

- 3 boneless, skinless chicken breasts (1-inch cubes)
- 1 tsp red onion, chopped
- 1 orange bell pepper, sliced
- 1 cup sliced yellow summer squash
- 4 tbsp of honey mustard salad dressing (divided)
- 1/2 tsp. dried thyme
- 1/2 pound mayonnaise
- 2 tablespoons lemon juice

Method:

1. In the air fryer basket, combine the chicken, onion, pepper, and squash.
2. Drizzle with 1 tablespoon of the honey mustard salad dressing, then stir with the herbs.
3. A food thermometer should read 165°F when the chicken is done cooking. Toss the chicken once during the cooking time.
4. In a mixing dish, combine the chicken and veggies with the remaining 3 tablespoons of honey mustard salad dressing, mayonnaise, and lemon juice. Serve on lettuce leaves if desired.

A tip for a variation:

Allow this salad to cool before using it as a filling for chicken salad sandwiches. Ciabatta rolls, croissants, or pita bread may be used.

Cost per serving:

494 calories; 23 grams total fat; 5 grams saturated fat; 159 milligrams cholesterol; 439 milligrams sodium, 18g of carbohydrates; 2g of fiber; 51g of protein

ASIAN TURKEY MEATBALLS

Preparation time: 10 minutes/Cooking time: 11 to 14 minutes/Serves 4

Preheat the oven to 400°F.

Family member's favorite

These turkey meatballs shine because of the Asian seasonings. To create tender meatballs, mix all of the ingredients before adding the meat.

Ingredients:

- split 2 tbsp. of peanut oil,
- 1 small onion, minced
- 1/4 cups of coarsely chopped water chestnuts
- 1/2 teaspoons of ginger powder
- 2 tbsp. of low-sodium soy sauce
- 1/4 cups of bread crumbs (panko)
- 1 egg, beaten
- 1 pound ground turkey

Method:

1. Combine the peanut oil and onion in a 6-by-6-by-2-inch pan. Cook for 1 to 2 minutes, or until the vegetables are crisp and tender. Place the onions in a medium mixing basin.
2. Mix in the water chestnuts, ground ginger, soy sauce, and bread crumbs with the onions. Stir in the egg well. Incorporate the ground turkey until well blended.
3. Make 1-inch meatballs out of the mixture. Drizzle the meatballs with the remaining 1 tablespoon of oil.
4. In batches, bake the meatballs in the 6-by-6-by-2-inch pan for 10 to 12 minutes, or until a meat thermometer reads 165°F.

Optional sauce: If desired, add a sauce. 1 cup chicken broth, 2 tablespoons cornstarch, and 1/2 cups pineapple juice. Place the meatballs in a 6-inch bowl and cover with the sauce. Bake for 4 to 6 minutes, or until the sauce has thickened. With steamed rice, serve.

Cost per serving:

336 calories; 21 grams total fat; 4 grams saturated fat; 157 milligrams cholesterol; 487 milligrams sodium, 34g protein; 8g carbohydrate; 1g fiber

CHICKEN WITH PINEAPPLE STIR-FRY

Preparation time: 10 minutes/Cooking time: 11 to 15 minutes/Serves 4

STIR-FRY 370°F

Family member's favorite

Stir-fried chicken is often covered with a cornstarch-egg white combination. This method is known as "velveting," and it results in an extraordinarily soft chicken. In this simple meal, chicken is paired with onions and pineapple. With steamed rice, serve.

Ingredients:

- 2 chicken breasts, skinless and boneless
- 2 tablespoons cornstarch
- 1 egg white, gently beaten
- 1 tablespoon olive or peanut oil
- 1 onion, sliced
- 1 red bell pepper, chopped
- 1 can (8 oz.) pineapple tidbits, drained, reserved juice
- 2 tbsp soy sauce (reduced sodium).

Method:

1. Cut the chicken breasts into cubes and place them in a medium mixing dish. Mix in the cornstarch and the egg white completely. Place aside.
2. Combine the oil and onion in a 6-inch metal bowl. Cook for 2 to 3 minutes in the air fryer, or until the onion is crisp and tender.
3. Drain the chicken and combine it with the onions in a mixing dish; toss thoroughly. Cook for 7 to 9 minutes, or until the chicken reaches an internal temperature of 165°F.
4. Toss the chicken mixture, and then stir in the pepper, pineapple tidbits, 3 tablespoons of the conserved pineapple juice, and soy sauce. Cook for 2 to 3 minutes, or until the food is cooked through and the sauce has thickened somewhat.

A suggestion for a substitution:

In this recipe, boneless, skinless chicken thighs may be substituted for the chicken breasts. Cook the thighs for 8 to 10 minutes, or until a meat thermometer reads 165°F.

Cost per serving:

291 calories; 9 grams total fat; 2 grams saturated fat; 101 milligrams cholesterol; 427 milligrams sodium, 16g of carbohydrates; 2g of fiber; 35g of protein

SWEET-AND-SOUR DRUMSTICKS

Preparation time: 5 minutes/Cooking time: 23 to 25 minutes/Serves 4

Bake at 350°F.

Family member's favorite:

Cooking chicken drumsticks in the air fryer is a two-step operation. First, the meat is fried until done, and then it is covered with a sweet-and-sour sauce and baked until glazed. The additional process results in a meal that is really unique.

Ingredients:

- 6 drumsticks of chicken.
- 3 tbsp. lemon juice, divided
- 3 tbsp. low-sodium soy sauce (split)
- 1 teaspoon of peanut oil.
- three tablespoons honey
- 3 tbsp brown sugar
- 2 tablespoons ketchup
- 1/4 cups of fresh pineapple juice

Method:

1. 1 tbsp lemon juice and 1 tbsp soy sauce on the drumsticks. Drizzle the peanut oil over the chicken in the air fryer basket. To coat, toss everything together. Bake the chicken for 18 minutes, or until it is nearly done.
2. Meanwhile, mix the remaining 2 tablespoons of lemon juice, remaining 2 tablespoons of soy sauce, honey, brown sugar, ketchup, and pineapple juice in a 6-inch bowl.
3. Add the cooked chicken to the bowl and swirl it around to thoroughly coat it with the sauce.

4. Insert the metal bowl into the basket. Cook for 5 to 7 minutes, or until the chicken is glazed and a meat thermometer reads 165°F.

A suggestion for a substitution:

This technique may be used to prepare boneless, skinless chicken breasts or thighs. Reduce the cooking time for the chicken breasts to 10 to 15 minutes and for the chicken thighs to 11 to 16 minutes.

Cost per serving: 242 calories; 7 grams of total fat; 2 grams of saturated fat; 61 milligrams of cholesterol; 804 milligrams of sodium, 20g protein; 25g carbohydrate; 0g fiber

SATAY CHICKEN

Preparation time: 12 minutes/Cooking time: 12 to 18 minutes/Serves 4

Grill 390°F

Family member's favorite:

Satay is an Indonesian meal comprised of skewered and grilled meat, generally chicken, with a spicy peanut sauce. The skewers are then cooked and served with extra peanut sauce for dipping.

Ingredients:

- 1/2 cups of peanut butter (crunchy)
- 1/3 cups of chicken broth
- Low-sodium soy sauce, 3 tbsp.
- 2 tablespoons lemon juice
- 2 minced garlic cloves.
- 2 tablespoons olive oil
- 1 teaspoon curry powder
- 1 pound of chicken tenders

Method:

1. In a medium mixing bowl, whisk together the peanut butter, chicken broth, soy sauce, lemon juice, garlic, olive oil, and curry powder until smooth. Two tablespoons of this mixture should be placed in a small bowl. Set aside the leftover sauce in a serving dish.
2. Stir the chicken tenders into the dish with the 2 tablespoons of sauce. Allow it to marinade for a few minutes before slicing using a bamboo slicing knife.

3. Insert a skewer lengthwise through each chicken tender.

4. Place the chicken in the air fryer basket and cook in batches for 6 to 9 minutes, or until a meat thermometer reads 165°F. Serve the chicken with the reserved sauce on the side.

A Tip for the Air Fryer:

As some of the sauce drips off the chicken, the air fryer may begin to smoke. If you want to reduce smoke, add a tablespoon or two of water to the pan linked to the basket.

Cost per serving: 448 calories; 28 grams total fat; 5 grams saturated fat; 97 milligrams cholesterol; 1,004 milligrams sodium, 8g carbohydrate, 2g fiber, 46g protein.

STIR-FRY WITH ORANGE CURRIED CHICKEN

Preparation time: 10 minutes/Cooking time: 16 to 19 minutes/Serves 4

STIR-FRY 370°F

FAVORITE OF THE GLUTEN-FREE FAMILY

This quick stir-fry dish is sweet and spicy thanks to the use of orange juice and curry powder. Serve over freshly cooked rice with a green salad for a great, easy supper.

Ingredients:

- 3/4-pound boneless, skinless chicken thighs cut into 1-inch chunks.
- 1 yellow bell pepper, diced into 1 1/2-inch cubes
- 1 tsp red onion, chopped
- Misting with olive oil
- 1/4-cup chicken broth
- 2 tablespoons honey
- 1/4 cc of orange juice
- 1 tsp corn starch
- 2 to 3 tablespoons curry powder

Method:

1. Mist the air fryer basket with olive oil before adding the chicken thighs, pepper, and red onion.

2. Cook for 12 to 14 minutes, or until the chicken reaches 165°F, shaking the basket halfway through.

3. Set aside the chicken and veggies from the air fryer basket.

4. Mix the stock, honey, orange juice, cornstarch, and curry powder in a 6-inch metal bowl. Stir in the chicken and veggies before placing the bowl in the basket.

5. Return the basket to the air fryer for another 2 minutes of cooking time. Remove from the heat and whisk for 2–3 minutes, or until the sauce thickens and becomes bubbly.

6. What Did You Know? Curry powder is not a single spice, but rather a blend of many spices. Each family in India creates their own mix.

Cost per serving:

230 calories; 7 grams of total fat; 2 grams of saturated fat; 76 milligrams of cholesterol; 124 milligrams of sodium, 26g protein; 2g fiber; 16g carbohydrate

STIR-FRY WITH SPICY CHICKEN

Preparation time: 10 minutes/Cooking time: 13 to 16 minutes/Serves 4

STIR-FRY 370°F

Gluten-Free

A stir-fry does not have to have an Asian flavor! This bright and exciting dish incorporates spicy Tex-Mex ingredients to make a quick and easy meal.

Ingredients:

- 2 chicken breasts, skinless and boneless
- 2 tablespoons cornstarch
- 2 tbsp of peanut oil
- 1 onion, sliced
- 1 jalapeo pepper, sliced
- 1 red bell pepper, chopped
- 1 pound frozen corn
- a 1/2 cup salsa

Method:

1. Chicken breasts should be cut into 1-inch chunks. In a shallow dish, toss the chicken in the cornstarch to coat. Set aside the chicken.

2. Combine the oil and onion in a 6-inch metal bowl. Cook for 2 to 3 minutes, or until the vegetables are crisp and tender.

3. Place the chicken in the mixing bowl. Cook for 7 to 8 minutes, or until almost done. Combine the jalapeo pepper, red bell pepper, corn, and salsa in a mixing bowl.
4. Cook, stirring occasionally, for 4 to 5 minutes, or until the chicken reaches 165°F and the veggies are crisp and tender. With steamed rice, serve.

Suggestion for an ingredient:

Salsa may be mild or spicy, depending on the kind of peppers used. Habanero and serrano peppers are the hottest. Jalapeo peppers are less spicy. Read labels carefully to ensure that you are purchasing the strength of salsa that you enjoy.

Cost per serving:

351 calories; 16 grams total fat; 4 grams saturated fat; 101 milligrams cholesterol; 296 milligrams sodium, 18g of carbohydrates; 3g of fiber; 35g of protein

FAJITAS DE POLLO (CHICKEN FAJITAS)

Preparation time: 10 minutes/Cooking time: 10 to 14 minutes/Serves 4

Preheat the grill to 380°F.

FAVORITE OF THE GLUTEN-FREE FAMILY

Fajitas are created with grilled chicken and vegetables, mixed in a spicy sauce, and served in a soft corn tortilla with avocados and lettuce. The spice level of the salsa you use may be used to modulate the heat of this meal.

Ingredients:

- 4 boneless, skinless chicken breasts, sliced
- 1 tsp red onion, chopped
- 2 sliced red bell peppers
- 1/2 cups of spicy ranch salad dressing
- 1/2 tsp. dried oregano
- 8 tortillas de maize.
- 2 cups butter lettuce, shredded
- Two peeled and sliced avocados

Method:

1. In the air fryer basket, combine the chicken, onion, and pepper. Drizzle with 1 tablespoon salad dressing and sprinkle with oregano. To mix, toss everything together.

2. Grill the chicken for 10 to 14 minutes or until it reaches 165°F on a foo thermometer.

3. Toss the chicken and veggies with the remaining salad dressing in a mixing bowl.

4. Serve the chicken mixture beside the tortillas, lettuce, and avocados, and let everyone build their own masterpieces.

A suggestion for a substitution:

In place of the chicken breasts in this recipe, you might substitute sliced boneless, skinless chicken thighs. The cooking time will be 12 to 17 minutes. **Longer**: Be careful to use a meat thermometer to check for doneness.

Cost per serving:

783 calories; 38 grams total fat; 9 grams saturated fat; 202 milligrams cholesterol; 397 milligrams sodium, 72g protein; 12g fiber; 39g carbohydrate

TURKEY TEX-MEX BURGERS

Preparation time: 10 minutes/Cooking time: 14 to 16 minutes/Serves 4

Preheat the grill to 330°F.

GLUTEN-FREE FAMILY FAVORITE

Turkey burgers are lower in fat than ground beef burgers. However, for food safety considerations, they must be cooked at 165°F until well-done. With the help of unusual tastes, dull turkey is transformed into something unforgettable in this dish!

Ingredients:

- 1/3 cup crumbled corn tortilla chips
- 1 egg, beaten
- a 1/4 cup salsa
- 1/3 cup pepper, Cheddar cheese, shredded
- A pinch of salt
- black pepper, freshly ground
- 1 pound turkey ground
- 1 tablespoon of olive oil
- 1 teaspoon paprika

Method:

1. In a medium mixing bowl, combine the tortilla chips, egg, salsa, cheese, salt, and pepper.

2. Mix in the turkey gently but completely with clean hands.
3. Form the meat mixture into 1/2 inch-thick patties. Make a thumb depression in the middle of each patty to prevent the burgers from puffing up during cooking.
4. Brush both sides of the patties with olive oil and sprinkle with paprika.
5. Place the air fryer basket in the air fryer. Grill the beef for 14 to 16 minutes, or until it reaches an internal temperature of at least 165°F.

A suggestion for a substitution:

If you choose, you may use ground chicken or ground pork for the ground beef in this recipe. Both would complement the tastes and textures.

Price per serving:

354 calories; 21 grams total fat; 5 grams saturated fat; 166 milligrams cholesterol; 337 milligrams sodium, 11g of carbohydrates, 2g of fiber, and 36g of protein

THIGHS OF BARBECUED CHICKEN

Preparation time: 10 minutes/Cooking time: 15 to 18 minutes/Serves 4

Preheat the grill to 380°F.

FAVORITE OF THE GLUTEN-FREE FAMILY

There are many fantastic barbecue sauces out there, but even the finest ones could need a bit of extra zip. Perform a taste test with a few brands to see which one you like. They might be spicy or sweet, hot or cold, thick or thin. Then add flavorings like garlic, herbs, or spices to the mix.

Ingredients:

- 6 chicken thighs, boneless and skinless
- 1/4-cup gluten-free barbecue sauce from the shop
- 2 minced garlic cloves.
- 2 tablespoons lemon juice

Method:

1. In a medium mixing bowl, combine the chicken, barbecue sauce, cloves, and lemon juice. Allow for a 10-minute marinating period.
2. Shake the chicken thighs out of the bowl to remove any excess sauce.
3. Place the chicken pieces in the air fryer, allowing some space between them.

4. Grill the chicken for 15 to 18 minutes, or until an instant read meat thermometer reads 165°F.

A Tip for the Air Fryer:

The air fryer may smoke somewhat when the sauce drips off the chicken while it cooks. That's OK; just check the chicken halfway through the cooking time to ensure it's not scorching.

Cost per serving:

351 calories; 13 grams total fat; 4 grams saturated fat; 151 milligrams cholesterol; 323 milligrams sodium, 0g fiber; 6g carbohydrate; 49g protein

CHICKEN FRIED IN BUTTERMILK

Preparation time: 7 minutes/Cooking time: 20 to 25 minutes/Serves 4

Temperature of the fryer: 370 °F

Family member's favorite:

Fried chicken is the most sumptuous of all fried dishes. However, many people avoid making it at home since frying chicken causes oil to spatter everywhere. And eating it on a regular basis is just unhealthy. With this fantastic modification, the air fryer comes to the rescue.

Ingredients:

- Six chicken thighs, drumsticks, and breasts.
- 1 cup all-purpose flour
- 2 teaspoons paprika
- A pinch of salt
- Freshly ground black pepper.
- 1/3 pound buttermilk
- Two eggs
- 2 tablespoons olive oil
- 1 1/2 cup bread crumbs

Method:

1. Dry the chicken with a towel. Combine the flour, paprika, salt, and pepper in a small basin.
2. In a separate dish, whisk together the buttermilk and eggs until smooth.

3. In a third dish, whisk together the olive oil and bread crumbs.
4. Dredge the chicken in flour, then in eggs, and lastly in bread crumbs, pushing the crumbs firmly onto the chicken skin.
5. Cook the chicken for 20 to 25 minutes, turning each piece over halfway through, or until the flesh registers 165°F on a meat thermometer.
6. The chicken is brown and crisp, according to the thermometer. Allow it to cool for 5 minutes before serving.

A tip for a variation:

Before cooking, marinate the chicken in buttermilk and spices such as cayenne pepper, chili powder, or garlic powder overnight. This increases the moistness and tenderness of the chicken while also adding flavor.

Cost per serving:

644 calories, 17g total fat, 4g saturated fat, 214mg cholesterol, 495mg sodium, 55g carbohydrate, 3g fiber, and 62g protein

CREAMY POTATOES WITH GARLIC-ROASTED CHICKEN

Preparation time: 10 minutes/Cooking time: 25 minutes/Serves 4

Preheat the oven to 380°F.

FAVORITE OF THE GLUTEN-FREE FAMILY

Yes, as long as it fits readily inside the air fryer basket, you may roast a full chicken in the air fryer. Choose a small broiler-fryer (approximately 3 pounds) for this recipe. It takes a little longer than 30 minutes from start to finish, but this is to ensure that the chicken is crisp on the exterior and juicy and soft on the inside.

Ingredients:

- 1 whole broiler-fryer chicken (2 1/2 to 3 pounds)
- 2 tablespoons olive oil
- 1/2 teaspoon garlic salt
- 8 garlic cloves, peeled
- 1 slice lemon
- 1/2 tsp. dried thyme
- 1/2 tsp. dried marjoram
- 1/2 to 16 scrubbed creamer potatoes.

Method:

1. Before cooking, do not wash the chicken. Remove the chicken from its package and pat it dry.
2. In a small bowl, combine the olive oil and salt. Half of this mixture should be applied to the interior of the bird, beneath the skin, and on the chicken skin.
3. Insert the garlic cloves and lemon slice into the cavity of the bird. Sprinkle the thyme and marjoram over the chicken.
4. Place the chicken in the basket of the air fryer. Surround them with the potatoes, then sprinkle with the remaining olive oil mixture.
5. After 25 minutes, check the temperature of the chicken. The temperature should be 160°F. Make sure the probe does not contact bone in the thickest area of the breast. Return the chicken to the air fryer and cook for 4 to 5 minutes, or until the temperature reaches 160°F.
6. When the chicken and potatoes are done, place them on a serving plate and cover with foil. Allow 5 minutes for the chicken to rest before serving.

Suggestions for an ingredient:

Creamer potatoes have tiny, spherical, white skins that are thin and delicate. They are often not peeled before cooking. In the vegetable section of the grocery store, you may occasionally find them in microwave-safe cartons.

Cost per serving:

491 calories; 14 grams total fat; 3 grams saturated fat; 175 milligrams cholesterol; 151 milligrams sodium, 68g protein; 20g carbohydrate; 3g fiber

CHICKEN CORDON BLEU CHICKEN CORDON BLEU

Preparation time: 15 minutes/Cooking time: 13 to 15 minutes/Serves 4

Temperature of the fryer: 380 °F

Family member's favorite

Cordon bleu is French for "blue ribbon," and it is also the name of a well-known Parisian cooking school. Chicken Cordon Bleu is chicken stuffed with ham and Swiss or Gruyère cheese. It's a gourmet dish that's a breeze to prepare in the air fryer.

Ingredients:

- 4 Filets of chicken breast

- 1/4-cup ham, diced
- 1/3 cup grated Gruyère or Swiss cheese
- 1/4 cups of flour
- A pinch of salt
- Freshly ground black pepper.
- 1/2 tsp. dried marjoram
- One egg
- 1 cup panko bread crumbs
- Misting with olive oil

Method:

1. Place the chicken breast filets on a work surface and gently press them with your palm to make them thinner. Do not rip the meat.
2. Combine the ham and cheese in a small bowl. Distribute the chicken filets with this mixture. To envelop the filling, wrap the chicken around it.
3. Toothpicks were used to keep the chicken together.
4. Combine the flour, salt, pepper, and marjoram in a small basin. In a separate dish, whisk the egg. On a dish, spread out the bread crumbs.
5. To fully coat the chicken, dip it in the flour mixture, then in the egg, and lastly in the bread crumbs.
6. Mist the chicken with olive oil and place it in the air fryer basket.
7. Bake for 13 to 15 minutes, or until the chicken reaches 165°F. Remove the toothpicks with care and serve.

Suggestions for an ingredient

Chicken filets, which are sliced from the chicken breast, may be found in most big supermarket shops. If you can't locate them, you may produce two thin slices by cutting one chicken breast in half and holding your knife parallel to the work surface.

Cost per serving:

478 calories; 12 grams total fat; 3 grams saturated fat; 200 milligrams cholesterol; 575 milligrams sodium. 2g fiber; 26g carbohydrate; 64g protein

CHICKEN BURGERS WITH HAM AND CHEESE STUFFING

Preparation time: 12 minutes/Cooking time: 13 to 16 minutes/Serves 4

Preheat the grill to 350°F.

Family member's favorite

This meal is a much more relaxed version of the original Chicken Cordon Bleu recipe. Serve these soft and juicy burgers on toasted onion buns smeared with mayonnaise and mustard and heaped with lettuce and sliced tomatoes.

Ingredients:

- 1/3-Cup Soft Bread Crusted
- three tablespoons milk
- 1 egg, beaten
- 1/2 tsp. dried thyme
- A pinch of salt
- Freshly ground black pepper.
- 1 1/4-pound chicken ground
- 1/4-cup ham, coarsely chopped
- 1 /3 cup grated Havarti cheese
- Misting with olive oil

Method:

1. Combine the bread crumbs, milk, egg, thyme, salt, and pepper in a medium mixing bowl. Mix in the chicken gently but completely with clean hands.
2. Place the chicken into eight thin patties on waxed paper.
3. Place the ham and cheese on top of four of the patties. On top of the remaining four patties, gently press the sides together to seal, ensuring that the ham and cheese mixture is in the center of the burger.
4. Mist the burgers with olive oil and place them in the basket. Grill for 13 to 16 minutes, or until the chicken reaches 165°F when tested with a meat thermometer.

Suggestions for an ingredient:

Many supermarkets sell pre-chopped ham in the meat area. However, for this dish, the ham should be cut into 1/4-inch slices. If the ham you purchase is bigger, cut it finer.

Cost per serving: 367 calories; 15 grams total fat; 5 grams saturated fat; 179 milligrams cholesterol; 370 milligrams sodium, 8g of carbohydrates; 1g of fiber; 47g of protein

TENDERS OF CHICKEN WITH VEGGIES

Preparation time: 10 minutes/Cooking time: 18 to 20 minutes/Serves 4

Preheat the oven to 380°F.

Family member's favorite:

In the air fryer, chicken tenders cook to perfection. You'll cover them in honey and seasoned bread crumbs in this recipe. On a weekday, serve this hearty meal with a green salad and garlic bread. It's a hit with kids!

Ingredients:

- 1 pound of chicken tenders
- 1 tablespoon honey
- A pinch of salt
- Freshly ground black pepper.
- 1/2 cup soft fresh bread crumbs
- 1/2 tsp. dried thyme
- 1 tablespoon of olive oil
- 2 carrots, sliced
- 12 red potatoes, tiny but

Method:

1. Toss the chicken tenders with the honey, salt, and pepper in a medium mixing basin Pepper.
2. Mix the bread crumbs, thyme, and olive oil in a small basin.
3. Coat the tenders with bread crumbs, pressing them firmly into the flesh.
4. In the air fryer basket, layer the carrots and potatoes with the chicken tenders.
5. Cook for 18 to 20 minutes, or until the chicken reaches 165°F and the veggies are tender, shaking the basket halfway through.

What Did You Know? When chicken tenders are served boneless and skinless, they are sliced from the chicken breast. The tender is a small muscle located behind the breast.

Cost per serving:

378 calories; 8 grams total fat; 1 gram saturated fat; 97 milligrams cholesterol; 296 milligrams sodium, 35g of carbohydrates; 3g of fiber; 41g of protein

MEAT RECIPES

STIR-FRY OF SPICY THAI BEEF

Preparation time: 15 minutes/Cooking time: 6 to 9 minutes/Serves 4

STIR-FRY 370°F

Gluten-Free:

This dish gets its characteristic Thai taste from peanut butter, red chilies, and lime juice. The delicate beef and broccoli, along with garlic, elevate this meal to the level of a feast.

Ingredients:

- 1 pound of thinly sliced sirloin steaks
- 2 tablespoons lime juice (divided)
- 1/3 cups of nutty peanut butter
- ½ pound of beef broth
- 1 tablespoon of olive oil
- Broccoli florets 1 1/2 cup
- Two garlic cloves, sliced
- 1 to 2 red Chile peppers, sliced

Method:

1. In a medium mixing dish, combine the steak and 1 tablespoon lime juice. Place aside.
2. In a small mixing dish, combine the peanut butter and beef broth.
3. Drain the meat and toss in the peanut butter mixture with the liquid from the bowl.
4. Combine the olive oil, steak, and broccoli in a 6-inch metal bowl. Cook, shaking the basket once during the cooking process, for 3–4 minutes, or until the steak is nearly done and the broccoli is crisp and tender.
5. Stir in the garlic, chili peppers, and peanut butter combination.
6. Cook, stirring occasionally, for 3 to 5 minutes, or until the sauce is boiling and the broccoli is cooked. With steamed rice, serve.

What Did You Know? The membranes and seeds of a chili pepper contain the heat. Leave them in if you want spicy cuisine, but remove and discard them if you like a bit less spice. Also, be careful when handling Chile peppers! When chopping peppers, never contact your eyes or lips since the chemical capsaicin in the peppers might burn your eyes.

Cost per serving:

387 calories; 22 grams total fat; 6 grams saturated fat; 101 milligrams cholesterol; 281 milligrams sodium, 7g of carbohydrates; 2g of fiber; 42g of protein

BURGERS IN THAI STYLE

Preparation time: 10 minutes/Cooking time: 15 minutes/Serves 4

Preheat the grill to 380°F.

Family member's favorite:

Did you know that ground beef, and all ground meat in general, must be cooked to 165°F for food safety reasons? Food poisoning is possible if the temperature is too low. It's possible to cook the burger perfectly while keeping it moist and juicy by putting bread crumbs and water in the meat, but that's not the only way.

Ingredients:

- 1/2 CUP TOASTED BAKED BREAD CRUMBS
- 1/4 tbsp. Thai chili sauce
- Two green onions, minced
- 2 minced garlic cloves.
- 1 1/4 pounds of 93 percent lean ground beef
- 4 onion rolls (cut in half)
- 1 large peeled and sliced beefsteak tomato
- 1/3 cups of store-bought peanut sauce

Method:

1. In a large mixing bowl, combine the bread crumbs, Thai chili sauce, green onions, and garlic. Add the ground beef and blend gently but thoroughly.
2. Make four patties out of the beef mixture. As the burgers cook, make a thumbhole in the middle of each one. This will keep the burgers from puffing up.
3. Cook for 12 minutes before testing the burgers. If they aren't at least 165°F, continue cooking for 3 minutes until they are.
4. Assemble the burgers with the onion rolls, tomato slices, and peanut sauce.

5. A suggestion for a substitution:
6. These burgers may be made using ground pork or a mix of ground pork and ground beef. When assembling the burgers, you might also add sliced onions and lettuce.

Cost per serving:

584 calories; 18 grams total fat; 5 grams saturated fat; 127 milligrams cholesterol; 1,315 milligrams sodium,53g protein; 3g fiber; 47g carbohydrate

KORMA DE BOEUF

Preparation time: 10 minutes/Cooking time: 17 to 20 minutes/Serves 4

Bake at 350°F.

Gluten-Free:

Beef korma is an Indian dish comprised of meat and vegetables that is cooked in a yogurt sauce seasoned liberally with curry powder. Depending on your preferences, it might be mild or spicy. Service with warm pita bread and a refreshing cucumber salad.

Ingredients:

- 1 pound sirloin steak, sliced
- 1/2-cup yoghurt
- 1 tablespoon curry powder
- 1 tablespoon of olive oil
- 1 onion, chopped
- 2 minced garlic cloves.
- 1 tomato, diced
- 1/2 cups of thawed frozen baby peas

Method:

- Combine the steak, yogurt, and curry powder in a medium mixing basin. Set it aside after stirring.
- Combine the olive oil, onion, and garlic in a 6-inch metal bowl. Cook for 3 to 4 minutes, or until the vegetables are crisp and tender.
- Combine the steak, yogurt, and chopped tomato in a mixing bowl. Cook for 12–13 minutes, or until the steak is almost tender.
- Cook for 2 to 3 minutes, or until the peas are heated through.

Suggestions for an ingredient:

Sirloin, sirloin tip, and top round are the finest cuts for this meal. Even with a little marinating time, the yogurt helps tenderize the meat.

Cost per serving:

298 calories; 11 grams total fat; 4 grams saturated fat; 103 milligrams cholesterol; 100 milligrams sodium,9g carbohydrate, 2g fiber, 38g protein.

STUFFED BELL PEPPERS WITH RICE AND MEATBALLS

Preparation time: 13 minutes/Cooking time: 11 to 17 minutes/Serves 4

Preheat the oven to 400°F.

FAVORITE OF THE GLUTEN-FREE FAMILY:

Stuffed peppers are a traditional comfort food. You may use whatever color of pepper you like. Mix and mix your peppers, then let your family vote on their favorite! For this recipe, use the mini appetizer-size meatballs. The quantity required is determined by the size of the peppers.

Ingredients:

- 4 red bell peppers.
- 1 tablespoon of olive oil
- 1 small onion, sliced
- 2 minced garlic cloves.
- 1 cup cooked frozen rice, thawed
- 16 to 20 thawed, tiny frozen precooked meatballs
- 1/2 pound tomato sauce
- A couple of tablespoons Mustard Dijon

Method:

1. Cut off approximately 1/2 inches of the tops of the peppers to prepare them. With care, remove the membranes and seeds from the insides of the peppers. Place aside.
2. Combine the olive oil, onion, and garlic in a 6-by-6-by-2-inch pan.
3. Bake for 2 to 4 minutes in the air fryer, or until crisp and tender. Set aside the vegetable mixture in a medium bowl after removing it from the pan.
4. Stir in the rice, meatballs, tomato sauce, and mustard to the vegetable mixture.
5. Fill the peppers halfway with the meat-vegetable mixture.

6. Bake for 9 to 13 minutes or until the filling is hot and the peppers are tender, in the air fryer basket.

Suggestions for an ingredient:

If you can't locate little meatballs that fit inside the bell peppers, purchase regular-size meatballs and chop them into thirds.

Cost per serving: 487 calories; 21 grams total fat; 7 grams saturated fat; 47 milligrams cholesterol; 797 milligrams sodium, Carbohydrates (57g), Fiber (6g), and Protein (26g)

STEAK AND CABBAGE STIR-FRY

Preparation time: 15 minutes/Cooking time: 8 to 13 minutes/Serves 4

STIR-FRY 370°F

Family member's favorite:

Cabbage provides a lot of flavor and nutrients to this simple yet filling recipe. In this dish, you may use either red or green cabbage, or a mixture of the two.

Ingredients:

- 1/2 lb. sirloin steak, thinly sliced
- 2 tbsp cornstarch
- 1 teaspoon of peanut oil.
- 2 cups chopped red or green cabbage
- 1 yellow bell pepper, chopped
- 2 green onions, chopped
- Two garlic cloves, sliced
- 1/2-cup stir-fry sauce (commercial)

Method:

1. Set aside the steak after tossing it with the cornstarch.
2. Combine the peanut oil and cabbage in a 6-inch metal bowl. Place it in the basket for 3 to 4 minutes.
3. Remove the bowl from the basket and fill it with the steak, pepper, onions, and garlic. Return the air fryer to the heat and cook for 3 to 5 minutes, or until the
4. The steak is cooked to your liking, and the veggies are crisp and delicate.
5. Cook for 2 to 4 minutes, or until the stir-fry sauce is hot. Serve it with rice.

A suggestion for a substitution:

Napa cabbage, a more typical stir-fry component, may be substituted for normal cabbage. You might also use bok Choy or broccoli florets.

Cost per serving:

180 calories; 7 grams of total fat; 2 grams of saturated fat; 51 milligrams of cholesterol; 1,843 milligrams of sodium,9g carbohydrate, 2g fiber, 20g protein.

CABBAGE, UNSTUFFED

Preparation time: 10 minutes/Cooking time: 14 to 20 minutes/Serves 4

Preheat the oven to 370°F.

FAVORITE OF THE GLUTEN-FREE FAMILY:

Traditional stuffed cabbage takes a lot of time and effort to prepare. Soften the cabbage leaves, prepare the filling, pack the cabbage, wrap it up, and bake it in sauce. This one-dish version of the recipe has the same flavor as the original but requires much less preparation.

Ingredients:

- 1 tablespoon of olive oil
- 1 small onion, sliced
- 1 1/2 cups of green cabbage, chopped
- 16 frozen precooked meatballs
- 1 cup frozen cooked rice
- Two tomatoes, chopped
- 1/2 tsp. dried marjoram
- A pinch of salt
- Freshly ground black pepper.

Method:

1. Combine the oil and onion in a 6-inch metal bowl. 2–4 minutes, or until the onion is crisp and soft.
2. Stir in the cabbage, meatballs, rice, tomatoes, marjoram, salt, and pepper.
3. Bake for 12 to 16 minutes or until the meatballs are hot, the rice is warmed, and the veggies are soft, stirring once throughout the cooking time.
4. Cooking hint
5. Most stores now provide prepared fresh vegetables that are ready to cook. Look in the vegetable department for chopped onions, cabbage for slaw, and other things like shredded carrots and sliced bell peppers.

<u>**Cost per serving:**</u>

453 calories; 20 grams total fat; 7 grams saturated fat; 47 milligrams cholesterol; 590 milligrams sodium,25g protein; 51g carbohydrate; 4g fiber

MEATBALLS WITH CHEESE STUFFING

Preparation time: 15 minutes/Cooking time: 10 to 13 minutes/Serves 4

Preheat the oven to 390°F.

<u>**Family member's favorite:**</u>

Meatballs packed with melted cheese are delicious! They're simple to create, albeit a little finicky. Feel free to use any kind of cheese that melts quickly in this recipe, from mozzarella to Swiss or Colby. Serve with spaghetti sauce on top of noodles or rice.

<u>**Ingredients:**</u>

- 1/3-Cup Soft Bread Crusted
- Three tablespoons milk
- 1 tablespoon ketchup
- One egg
- 1/2 tsp. dried marjoram
- A pinch of salt
- Freshly ground black pepper.
- 1 pound of 95 percent lean ground beef
- Twenty 1/2-inch cheese cubes
- Misting with olive oil

<u>**Method:**</u>

1. In a large mixing bowl, combine the bread crumbs, milk, ketchup, egg, marjoram, salt, and pepper.
2. Mix in the ground beef slowly but completely with your hands.
3. Make 20 meatballs out of the mixture.
4. Each meatball should be shaped around a cheese cube. Spray the meatballs with olive oil and place them in the air fryer basket.
5. Bake the meatballs for 10 to 13 minutes, or until a meat thermometer reads 165°F.

<u>**Cooking hint:**</u>

To create the best meatballs or meatloaf, combine all of the "filler" elements first, such as bread crumbs and eggs, before mixing in the meat. The more you work with the meat, the harder the meatballs get. To get the best results, handle ground beef as little as possible.

Cost per serving: 393 calories; 17 grams total fat; 8 grams saturated fat; 166 milligrams cholesterol; 499 milligrams sodium, 50g protein; 10g carbohydrate; 0g fiber

SPICY TOMATO SAUCE MEATBALLS

Preparation time: 10 minutes/Cooking time: 11 to 15 minutes/Serves 4

Preheat the oven to 400°F.

Family member's favorite:

Meatballs may become your go-to air fryer dish: You can cook juicy meatballs with a little crunchy crust in much less time than you would on the burner. Use ground beef that is at least 95% lean to prevent smoking.

Ingredients:

- 3 green onions, minced
- 1 garlic clove, minced
- 1 quail egg yolk
- 1/4 cups of crumbs from saltine crackers
- A pinch of salt
- Freshly ground black pepper.
- 1 pound of 95 percent lean ground beef
- Misting with olive oil
- 1 1/4 cups of spaghetti sauce (from a 16-ounce jar)
- A couple of tablespoons Mustard Dijon

Method:

1. Mix together the green onions, garlic, egg yolk, cracker crumbs, salt, and pepper in a large mixing basin.
2. Mix in the ground beef gently but completely with your hands until everything is mixed. Form the meatballs into 1 1/2-inch balls.
3. Mist the meatballs with olive oil and place them in the air fryer basket.
4. Bake for 8 to 11 minutes, or until the meatballs reach a temperature of 165°F.
5. Place the meatballs in a 6-inch metal dish after removing them from the basket.
6. Gently whisk in the spaghetti sauce and Dijon mustard.

7. 3 to 4 minutes, or until the sauce is thoroughly heated

A suggestion for a substitution:

These meatballs may be made using lean ground pig, ground chicken, ground turkey, or a mix of any of those meats. To ensure food safety, heat them until they record an internal temperature of 165°F.

Cost per serving:

360 calories; 12 grams of total fat; 4 grams of saturated fat; 154 milligrams of cholesterol; 875 milligrams of sodium, 39g protein; 24g carbohydrate; 3g fiber

MEXICO'S PIZZA

Preparation time: 10 minutes/Cooking time: 7 to 9 minutes/Serves 4

Preheat the oven to 370°F.

Family member's favorite

You may be shocked to hear that the air fryer bakes pizza beautifully — and fast! The crust crisps up, the cheese melts to perfection, and the toppings heat up but do not go mushy. This dish adds a spicy touch to a traditional pie.

Ingredients:

- Refried beans, 3/4 cups (from a 16-ounce can)
- 1/2 cup of salsa
- Frozen and sliced 10 frozen, precooked beef meatballs
- 1 jalapeo pepper, sliced
- Four pita breads (whole wheat)
- 1 cup shredded pepper Jack cheese
- 1/2 cups of Colby cheese, shredded
- 1/3-cup soured cream

Method:

1. Combine the refried beans, salsa, meatballs, and jalapeo pepper in a medium mixing basin.
2. Preheat the air fryer for 3–4 minutes or until it reaches a temperature of 350°F.
3. Sprinkle the cheeses over the pitas and top with the refried bean mixture.
4. Bake for 7–9 minutes, or until the crust is crisp and the cheese is melted and beginning to color.

5. Serve warm with a dollop of sour cream on top of each pizza.

A suggestion for a substitution:

You may add cooked pork sausage to this recipe if you like. Alternatively, add additional veggies to the refried bean mixture, such as mushrooms, chopped onion, or chopped tomatoes.

Cost per serving:

510 calories; 24 grams total fat; 12 grams saturated fat; 64 milligrams cholesterol; 1,196 milligrams sodium, 50g carbs; 9g fiber; 31g protein

STEAK TEX-MEX

Preparation time: 25 minutes/Cooking time: 20 minutes/Serves 4

Grill 390°F

Gluten-Free:

When you have an air fryer, you don't need a barbecue. From start to finish, this dish takes more than 30 minutes, but it's well worth the wait. It has the characteristic spicy taste of Mexican meals, with chipotle chiles and red pepper flakes giving it a kick.

Ingredients:

- 1 pound skirt steak
- 1 minced chipotle pepper in adobo sauce (La Costena or another gluten-free brand).
- 2 teaspoons of adobo sauce (La Costena or another gluten-free brand)
- 1/2 teaspoons of salt
- 1/8 teaspoon ground black pepper
- 1/8 teaspoons of red pepper flakes, crushed

Method:

1. Place the steak on a platter and cut it into four pieces.
2. Combine the minced chipotle pepper, adobo sauce, salt, pepper, and crushed red pepper flakes in a small bowl. Spread evenly over both sides of the steaks.
3. Allow the steaks to rest at room temperature for at least 20 minutes before serving, or refrigerate for up to 12 hours.
4. Grill the steaks in the air fryer basket, two at a time, for 10 minutes, or until they reach an internal temperature of at least 145°F. Repeat with the additional steaks while the first ones are resting, wrapped in foil.

5. Combine the freshly cooked steaks with the ones that have been resting for 5 minutes. To serve, slice thinly across the grain.

Suggestions for an ingredient:

Chipotles in adobo are jalapeo peppers roasted and jarred in a fiery red sauce. Many adobo sauces include gluten; thus, check the labels carefully or use the gluten-free La Costena brand.

Cost per serving:

244 calories; 11 grams total fat; 4 grams saturated fat; 67 milligrams cholesterol; 617 milligrams sodium,30g protein; 3g carbohydrate; 0g fiber

STEAK WITH FRENCH FRIES

Preparation time: 15 minutes/Cooking time: 15 minutes/Serves 4

Preheat the oven to 350°F.

Family member's favorite:

There is no chicken in a "chicken-fried" steak! It's basically a fried chicken-style technique for cooking steak. The steak is battered and deep-fried until it is crisp on the exterior and juicy on the inside. Because a batter alone would not produce the proper crust in an air fryer, bread crumbs are added to the mix.

Ingredients:

- (4 beef cube steaks, 6 oz.)
- 1/2 gallon buttermilk
- 1 cup all-purpose flour
- 2 teaspoons paprika
- 1 teaspoon garlic powder
- One egg
- 1 cup soft bread crumbs
- 2 tablespoons olive oil

Method:

1. Place the cube steaks on a plate or cutting board and pound them gently until they are somewhat thinner. Place aside.
2. Combine the buttermilk, flour, paprika, garlic salt, and egg in a small basin until barely mixed.

3. Mix the bread crumbs and olive oil together in a dish.
4. Coat the steaks in the buttermilk batter and let them sit for 5 minutes.
5. Bread crumbs should be used to coat the steaks. Pat the crumbs onto both sides of the steaks to completely coat them.
6. Air-fry the steaks for 12 to 16 minutes or until the meat thermometer reads 160°F and the coating is golden and crisp. This dish goes well with warm beef gravy.

What Did You Know? Cube steaks have been "mechanically tenderized" and must be grilled to medium-rare or well done. The meat has been punctured with needles or blades to tear up the fibers and make it soft when cooked. This also suggests that microorganisms on the meat's surface have made their way inside. For safety reasons, cook this sort of steak to 160°F.

Cost per serving:

630 calories; 21 grams of total fat; 6 grams of saturated fat; 194 milligrams of cholesterol; 358 milligrams of sodium,46g carbs; 3g fiber; 61g protein

COUNTRY RIBS THAT ARE TENDER

Preparation time: 5 minutes/Cooking time: 20 to 25 minutes/Serves 4

Preheat the oven to 400°F.

FAVORITE OF THE GLUTEN-FREE FAMILY:

Country-style pork ribs have higher meat content than spareribs. They may be purchased with or without the bone. Choose boneless ribs for this dish. The depth of flavor of traditional ribs is achieved in a fraction of the time when cooked in an air fryer.

Ingredients:

- 12 country-style pork ribs, skinned and trimmed.
- 2 tablespoons cornstarch
- 2 tablespoons olive oil
- 1 teaspoon dry mustard
- 1/2 teaspoons of fresh thyme
- 1/2 tablespoon garlic powder
- 1 teaspoon dried marjoram
- A pinch of salt
- Freshly ground black pepper.

Method:

- Lay the ribs out on a clean work surface.
- Combine the cornstarch, olive oil, mustard, thyme, garlic powder, marjoram, salt, and pepper in a small dish and massage into the ribs.
- Roast the ribs in the air fryer basket for 10 minutes.
- Turn the ribs carefully with tongs and continue to roast for 10 to 15 minutes, or until crisp and an internal temperature of at least 150 °F is recorded.

A Tip for the Air Fryer:

When turning the ribs, remove any extra fat from the air fryer pan that is underneath the basket. Place the pan and basket on a heatproof surface and gently press the basket release button. Drain the grease from the pan and replace the basket. Reattach the pan and resume cooking.

Cost per serving:

578 calories; 44 grams total fat; 14 grams saturated fat; 1153 milligrams cholesterol; 155 milligrams sodium, 40g protein; 4g carbohydrate; 0g fiber

PIZZA WITH BACON AND GARLIC

Time To Prepare: 10 Minutes/Time To Cook: 20 Minutes/Serves 4

Preheat the oven to 370°F.

Family member's favorite

Individual pizza crusts may be made using frozen dinner rolls. This dough is firmer than typical pizza dough in tubes, resulting in a crispier crust. By shaping the pizza into an oval, you can bake two at a time, allowing you to get dinner on the table faster.

Ingredients:

- For dusting, use flour.
- Flour-based nonstick baking spray
- 4 frozen large whole-wheat dinner rolls, thawed
- 5 garlic cloves, minced
- one-quarter cup pizza sauce
- 1/2 tsp. dried oregano
- 1/2 teaspoon garlic salt
- 8 precooked bacon slices, sliced into 1-inch pieces.
- 1 1/2 pound Cheddar cheese, shredded

Method:

1. Press each dinner roll into a 5-by-3-inch oval on a lightly floured board.
2. Place one crust on each of four 6-by-4-inch sheets of heavy-duty foil sprayed with nonstick spray.
3. Bake for 2 minutes, two at a time, or until the crusts are firm but not browned.
4. Meanwhile, mix the garlic, pizza sauce, oregano, and garlic salt in a small bowl. When the pizza crusts are done, sprinkle some of the sauce on top of each one. Garnish with bacon and cheddar cheese if desired.
5. Bake for another 8 minutes, two at a time or until the crust is browned and the cheese is melted and beginning to color.

A suggestion for a substitution:

This recipe may be used to make almost any pizza you want. Instead of bacon, use pepperoni. In lieu of the cheddar, use Swiss or mozzarella cheese. Add whatever vegetables you prefer, such as sliced mushrooms or chopped green onions.

Cost per serving: Total Fat: 42g; Saturated Fat: 19g; Cholesterol: 102mg; Sodium: 1250mg, 1,685mg; 53g carbohydrate; 3g fiber; 37g protein

POLISH SAUSAGE WITH A SWEET AND SOUR FLAVOR

Preparation time: 10 minutes/Cooking time: 10 to 15 minutes/Serves 4

Preheat the oven to 350°F.

Family member's favorite

Polish sausage cooks beautifully in an air fryer. Even when sliced into pieces before cooking, the exterior crisps up and the interior remains moist and delicious. This sausage becomes a substantial evening meal when cooked in a sweet-and-sour sauce with veggies. Serve it with rice.

Ingredients:

- 3/4 pounds of Polish sausage.
- 1 peeled and sliced red bell pepper into 1-inch strips
- 1/2 cups of finely chopped onions
- 3 tbsp brown sugar
- 1/3 cups of ketchup
- 2 tablespoons mustard
- 2 tablespoons apple cider vinegar

- 1/2 cups of chicken broth (about

Method:

1. Place the sausage in a 6-inch metal dish and cut it into 1 1/2-inch pieces.
2. Combine the pepper and chopped onion in a mixing bowl.
3. Combine the brown sugar, ketchup, mustard, apple cider vinegar, and chicken broth in a small mixing basin. Pour into the mixing bowl.
4. 10 to 15 minutes or until the sausage is hot, the veggies are soft, and the sauce is boiling and slightly thickened.

What Did You Know? Polish sausage is nearly always supplied completely cooked; check the label carefully to ensure that you choose a fully cooked kind for this recipe. Uncooked sausages are too fatty and produce too much oil to be cooked in this machine.

Cost per serving:

381 calories; 26 grams total fat; 8 grams saturated fat; 71 milligrams cholesterol; 957 milligrams sodium, 17g carbohydrate, 2g fiber, 19g protein.

LEMON PORK TENDERLOIN

Preparation time: 5 minutes/Cooking time: 10 minutes/Serves 4

Preheat the oven to 400°F.

FAMILY FAVORITE, GLUTEN-FREE:

Pork tenderloin is one of the most delicate slices of meat since it originates from a seldom utilized region of the animal near the rib cage. It absorbs flavors rapidly and cooks fast, allowing you to have supper on the table in minutes.

Ingredients:

- 1 pound pork tenderloin, cut into 1/2" slices
- 1 tablespoon of olive oil
- 1 teaspoon fresh lemon juice
- 1 tablespoon honey
- 1/2 teaspoon lemon zest
- 1/2 tsp. dried marjoram
- A pinch of salt
- Freshly ground black pepper.

Method:

- In a medium mixing dish, combine the pork tenderloin pieces.
- Combine the olive oil, lemon juice, honey, lemon zest, and salt in a small mixing basin.
- Salt, pepper, and marjoram. Combine everything.
- Pour the marinade over the tenderloin slices and rub it in lightly with your fingertips.
- Place the pork in the air fryer basket and cook for 10 minutes, or until a meat thermometer reads at least 145°F.

Suggestions for an ingredient:

Pre-marinated pork tenderloin is often available in supermarkets, making this meal even easier to cook. Simply slice the pork loin and cook it for 10 minutes, and you'll be ready to eat!

Cost per serving:

209 calories; 8 grams total fat; 2 grams saturated fat; 83 milligrams cholesterol; 104 milligrams sodium, 30g protein; 5g carbohydrate; 0g fiber

TENDERLOIN OF CRISPY MUSTARD PORK

Preparation time: 10 minutes/Cooking time: 14 minutes/Serves 4

390°F FRYING

Family member's favorite

The tenderloin of pork is the tenders cut of the pig. This beef crisps up on the exterior while remaining juicy on the inside after being covered with mustard and chopped garlic, then bread crumbs. Serve with roasted potatoes and a fruit salad for a filling meal.

Ingredients:

- 1 pound of pork tenderloin, sliced into 1-inch thick slices.
- A pinch of salt
- Freshly ground black pepper.
- A couple of tablespoons Mustard Dijon
- 1 garlic clove, minced
- 1/2 tsp. dried basil
- 1 cup soft bread crumbs
- 2 tablespoons olive oil

Method:

- Pound the pork pieces gently until they are about 3/4 inches thick.
- Season both sides with salt and pepper.
- Coat the pork with Dijon mustard and season with garlic and basil.
- Mix the bread crumbs and olive oil together in a dish. Coat the pork slices in the bread crumbs mixture, pressing them down to ensure the crumbs adhere.
- Fill the air fryer basket halfway with pork, allowing a little space between each piece. Air-fry for 12 to 14 minutes or until the pork reaches an internal temperature of at least 145°F.
- A meat thermometer reads 145°F, and the coating is crisp and golden. Serve immediately.

Suggestions for an ingredient:

When shopping for pork tenderloin, be sure to check the label. This cut is often offered marinated, and you don't want the marinade's flavors to clash with the seasonings in this dish. Look for basic tenderloin that has not been marinated for this dish.

Cost per serving: 335 calories; 13 grams of total fat; 3 grams of saturated fat; 83 milligrams of cholesterol; 390 milligrams of sodium

20g of carbohydrates; 2g of fiber; 34g of protein

VEGETABLES AND SIDES

MÉLANGE OF VEGETABLES WITH HERBS

Preparation time: 10 minutes/Cooking time: 14 to 18 minutes/Serves 4

Preheat the oven to 350°F.

GLUTEN-FREE, VEGAN

Roasted veggies go well with practically any dish, whether it's a grilled steak, roasted chicken, or hamburgers. Choose delicate vegetables for this dish so that they cook at the same pace.

Ingredients:

- 1 red bell pepper, sliced
- 1 pound (8 ounces) sliced mushrooms
- 1 yellow summer squash, sliced
- 3 sliced garlic cloves
- 1 tablespoon of olive oil
- 1/2 tsp. dried thyme
- 1/2 tsp. dried basil
- 1/2 tsp. dried tarragon

Method:

1. In a medium mixing bowl, combine the pepper, mushrooms, squash, and garlic with the olive oil. Mix in the thyme, basil, and tarragon, and then toss one more time.
2. Fill the air fryer basket halfway with veggies. Roast the veggies for 14 to 18 minutes, or until tender.
3. When using dried herbs in an air fryer recipe, whether for roasted veggies or chicken, they must adhere to the meal; otherwise, they will just blow around in the air fryer and burn. Always cover vegetables or meat with a little oil before adding herbs; this ensures that the herbs remain in the dish and flavor it.

Cost per serving: 63 calories; 4 grams total fat; 1 gram saturated fat; 0 milligrams cholesterol; 10 milligrams sodium, 6 g carbohydrate, 2 g fiber, and 3 g protein

STEAMED GREEN VEGGIE TRIO

Preparation time: 6 minutes/Cooking time: 9 minutes/Serves 4

STEAM 330°F

QUICK, GLUTEN-FREE, AND VEGAN

This vegetable combination is tasty and timeless, and it can be cooked at any time of year. Fresh broccoli and green beans are accessible all year, while frozen peas are always available at the shop. Serve it as a colorful side dish with a steak or roasted chicken breast.

Ingredients:

- 2 cups broccoli florets
- Green beans, 1 pound
- 1 tablespoon of olive oil
- 1 teaspoon fresh lemon juice
- 1 cup frozen baby peas, thawed
- 2 tablespoons honey mustard
- A pinch of salt
- freshly ground black pepper.

Method:

1. Place the broccoli and green beans in the air fryer basket. In the air fryer pan, add 2 tablespoons of water. Toss the veggies in the olive oil and lemon juice to coat.
2. After 6 minutes of steaming, remove the basket from the air fryer and add the peas.
3. Steam the veggies for 3 minutes, or until they are hot and tender.
4. Transfer the veggies to a serving plate and top with the honey mustard, salt, and pepper. Toss everything together and serve.

Suggestions for an ingredient

Remove the florets off the stalk to prepare the broccoli. You may freeze the stem to use later in stir-fries. To prepare green beans, chop off both ends and thoroughly rinse them.

Cost per serving:

99 calories; 4g fat; 1g saturated fat; 0mg cholesterol; 95mg sodium, 13 g carbohydrate, 4 g fiber, and 4 g protein

CARROTS WITH GARLIC AND SESAME

Preparation time: 5 minutes/Cooking time: 16 minutes/Serves 4 to 6

Preheat the oven to 380°F.

FAMILY FAVORITE VEGAN AND GLUTEN-FREE

Carrots are loved by almost every youngster, but adults find them tedious.

Not with these carrots! The air fryer brings out the sweetness in this vegetable, and the texture is really divine: soft and a little chewy.

If your children dislike garlic, just leave it out of the dish.

Ingredients:

- 1 pound baby carrots
- 1 tablespoon sesame seed oil
- 1/2 tsp. dried dill
- A pinch of salt
- Freshly ground black pepper.
- 6 garlic cloves, peeled
- Sesame seeds, 3 tbsp.

Method:

1. In a medium mixing basin, combine the tiny carrots. Drizzle with sesame oil, and then mix with the dill, salt, and pepper to coat well.
2. Place the carrots in the air fryer basket. Cook for 8 minutes, shaking the basket once during the process.
3. Place the garlic cloves in the air fryer. Roast for 8 minutes or until the garlic and carrots are gently browned, shaking the basket once while cooking.
4. Before serving, transfer the dish to a serving dish and top with sesame seeds.

A tip for a variation:

Large carrots, chopped into bits, may be used in lieu of the tiny carrots in this recipe. You may also roast other root veggies like parsnips or rutabagas.

Cost per serving:

7g total fat; 1g saturated fat; 0 mg cholesterol; 129 mg sodium, 2g protein; 4g fiber; 13g carbohydrate

GARLIC-ROASTED BELL PEPPERS

Preparation time: 8 minutes/Cooking time: 22 minutes/Serves 4

Preheat the oven to 330°F.

FAMILY FAVORITE VEGAN AND GLUTEN-FREE

A vibrant array of roasted bell peppers is not only eye-catching, but also tasty and nutritious. You may use any kind of bell pepper that you find in the store. Serving with meatloaf makes a complete supper.

Ingredients:

- 1 red bell pepper, small
- 1 yellow bell pepper, small
- 1 orange bell pepper, small
- 1 green bell pepper, small
- 2 tbsp of olive oil (divided)
- 1/2 tsp. dried marjoram
- A pinch of salt
- Freshly ground black pepper.
- 1 garlic bulb

Method:

1. The bell peppers should be cut into 1-inch pieces.
2. Toss the bell peppers with 1 tablespoon of the oil in a large mixing dish.
3. Toss in the marjoram, salt, and pepper, and toss once more.
4. Remove the garlic head's top and lay the cloves on an oiled square of aluminum foil. Drizzle with the rest of the olive oil. Wrap the garlic in aluminum foil.
5. Place the wrapped garlic in the air fryer for 15 minutes before adding the bell peppers. Roast for 7 minutes or until the peppers and garlic are tender. Place the peppers in a serving dish.
6. Unwrap the foil and remove the garlic from the air fryer. When the garlic cloves are cool enough to handle, squeeze them out of the papery peel and combine them with the bell peppers.

Cooking hint:

To quickly remove the seeds from a bell pepper, use a sharp knife to cut around the stem and simply take off the stem with the seeds attached. Remove any stray seeds from the pepper and chop it into strips.

Cost per serving:

108 calories; 7 grams of total fat; 1 gram of saturated fat; 0 mg cholesterol; 45 milligrams of sodium, 10 g carbohydrate, 3 g fiber, and 2 g protein

ROASTED BRUSSELS SPROUTS

Preparation time: 8 minutes/Cooking time: 20 minutes/Serves 4

Preheat the oven to 330°F.

GLUTEN-FREE, VEGETARIAN

Because Brussels sprouts may be bitter, many people dislike them. However, when fried in the air fryer till golden and crisp, these little cabbages become delicate and delicious. Serve with garlic-roasted chicken (recipe here) for a filling feast.

Ingredients:

- 1 pound fresh Brussels sprouts
- 1 tablespoon of olive oil
- 1/2 teaspoons of salt
- 1/8 teaspoon ground black pepper
- 1/4 cups of Parmesan cheese, grated

Method:

1. Trim the Brussels sprouts' bottoms and remove any yellowing leaves. Toss the vegetables with the olive oil, salt, and pepper before placing them in the air frying basket.
2. Roast the Brussels sprouts for 20 minutes, shaking the air fryer basket twice while frying, until they are dark golden brown and crisp.
3. Toss the Brussels sprouts with the Parmesan cheese in a serving dish. Serve it right away.

What Did You Know? Brussels sprouts were first grown in Rome and were brought to the United States in the 1880s. The majority of Brussels sprouts farmed in the United States are grown in California.

Cost per serving:

102 calories; 5 grams of total fat; 2 grams of saturated fat; 5 milligrams of cholesterol; 385 milligrams of sodium,6g protein; 4g fiber; 11g carbohydrate

SWEET POTATOES WITH A SAVORY ROAST

Preparation time: 5 minutes/Cooking time: 25 minutes/Serves 4

Preheat the oven to 330°F.

FAMILY FAVORITE VEGETARIAN, GLUTEN-FREE

In the famous Christmas dish, sweet potatoes are cooked with brown sugar and topped with marshmallows. Have you ever tried making them with savory ingredients? This simple dish goes particularly well with meatloaf or pot roast.

Ingredients:

- 2 sweet potatoes, peeled and cut into 1-inch pieces
- 1 tablespoon of olive oil
- A pinch of salt
- Freshly ground black pepper.
- 1/2 tsp. dried thyme
- 1/2 tsp. dried marjoram
- 1/4 cups of Parmesan cheese, grated

Method:

1. Drizzle the olive oil over the sweet potato cubes in the air fryer basket. Gently toss. Mix in the salt, pepper, thyme, and marjoram, and toss one more time.
2. Cook for 20 minutes, shaking the air fryer basket once throughout the process.
3. Remove the basket from the air fryer and give the potatoes another shake.
4. Return to the air fryer and evenly sprinkle with the Parmesan cheese.
5. For 5 minutes, or until the potatoes are soft.

What Did You Know? Sweet potatoes and yams are two varieties of root vegetables. A genuine yam is a starchy white root vegetable that is popular in Caribbean cuisine. Sweet potatoes are abundant in vitamin A and often have a brilliant orange hue.

Cost per serving:

186 calories; 5 grams of total fat; 2 grams of saturated fat; 5 milligrams of cholesterol; 115 milligrams of sodium

4g protein; 5g fiber; 32g carbohydrate

FRENCH FRIES WITH CRISPY PARMESAN

Preparation time: 5 minutes/Cooking time: 10 minutes/Serves 4

390°F FRYING

FAMILY FAVORITE, VEGETARIAN AND GLUTEN-FREE

You may, of course, cook French fries in the air fryer using raw whole potatoes, but this will add 10 to 15 minutes to the preparation time. While the fries are still hot, they are covered with parmesan and herbs, which adds a tremendous depth of flavor.

Ingredients:

- 4 cups frozen thin French fries
- 2 tbsp extra-virgin olive oil
- 1/3 cup grated Parmesan cheese
- 1/2 tsp. dried thyme
- 1/2 tsp. dried basil
- 1/2 teaspoons of salt

Method:

1. Remove any ice that has formed on the French fries. Drizzle the olive oil over the French fries in the air fryer basket. Gently toss.
2. Cook for 10 minutes, or until the fries are golden brown and heated through, shaking the basket once throughout the frying time.
3. Place the fries in a serving bowl and immediately top with the Parmesan, thyme, basil, and salt. Serve right away. To coat.

Suggestions for an ingredient:

Russet potatoes are ideal for creating French fries because they have low moisture content and bake up soft and crisp. You may use red potatoes or Yukon gold potatoes, but the results will not be as crisp.

Cost per serving:

152 calories; 4 grams of total fat; 2 grams of saturated fat; 6 milligrams of cholesterol; 382 milligrams of sodium, 5g protein; 4g fiber; 24g carbohydrate

SCALLOPED POTATOES

Preparation time: 5 minutes/Cooking time: 20 minutes/Serves 4

Preheat the oven to 380°F.

Family member's favorite

Rich scalloped potatoes are simple to make in the air fryer and require just a few ingredients. You may replace the heavy cream with half-and-half or whole milk, but the result will be a less creamy side dish.

Ingredients:

- 2 cups pre-sliced refrigerated potatoes
- 3 garlic cloves, minced
- A pinch of salt
- Freshly ground black pepper.
- A quarter-cup of heavy cream

Method:

1. In a 6-by-6-by-2-inch baking sheet, layer the potatoes, garlic, salt, and pepper. Pour the cream over everything slowly.
2. Bake for 15 minutes, or until the potatoes are golden brown and soft on top. Check their condition and, if necessary, bake for 5 minutes, or until browned.
3. After around 10 minutes of baking time, sprinkle the cheese on top of the potatoes. Bake until the cheese is bubbling and beginning to brown, about 2/3 cups of shredded Swiss, Havarti, or Gouda.

Cost per serving:

133 calories; 8 grams of total fat; 5 grams of saturated fat; 31 milligrams of cholesterol; 52 milligrams of sodium, 2g protein; 2g fiber; 13g carbohydrate

SALAD WITH ROASTED POTATOES

Preparation time: 5 minutes/Cooking time: 25 minutes/Serves 4 to 6

Preheat the oven to 350°F.

FAMILY FAVORITE VEGETARIAN, GLUTEN-FREE

Potato salad is a flexible meal that may be served at any time of year. This salad is served warm, but it may be chilled and enjoyed later. The lemony dressing will be absorbed by the heated potatoes.

Ingredients:

- 2 pounds, cut-in-half, of little red or white potatoes
- 1 tablespoon + 1/3 cups olive oil
- A pinch of salt
- Freshly ground black pepper.
- 1 red bell pepper, chopped
- 2 green onions, chopped
- 1 quart lemon juice
- 3 tbsp Dijon mustard or yellow mustard?

Method:

1. Drizzle 1 tablespoon of olive oil over the potatoes in the air fryer basket. Season with salt and pepper to taste.
2. Roast the potatoes for 25 minutes, tossing them twice during the cooking time, until they are soft and have a light golden brown color.
3. In the meantime, combine the bell pepper and green onions in a large mixing bowl.
4. In a small mixing bowl, whisk together the remaining 1/3 cup of olive oil, lemon juice, and mustard.
5. When the potatoes are done, combine them with the bell peppers in a mixing dish and drizzle with the dressing. To coat, toss everything together. Allow for a 20-minute cooling period. Stir gently once more before serving, or chill and serve later.

A tip for a variation:

This recipe may be brightened and made more complicated by adding a generous amount of fresh chopped herbs. Depending on your preferences, try chopped dill, basil, or rosemary. The warmth of the potatoes will intensify the taste of the herbs.

Cost per serving: 353 calories; 21 grams total fat; 3 grams saturated fat; 0 milligrams cholesterol; 192 milligrams sodium, 5g protein; 7g fiber; 39g carbohydrate

A CASEROLE OF CREAMY CORN

Preparation time: 5 minutes/Cooking time: 15 minutes/Serves 4

Preheat the oven to 320°F.

A Vegetarian Family Favorite:

A corn casserole is a hearty and homely side dish that goes well with meatloaf or roasted chicken. When fried in the air fryer, this traditional meal comes together fast.

Ingredients:

- Flour-based nonstick baking spray
- 2 cups frozen yellow corn
- Three tablespoons flour
- 1 egg, beaten
- 1/4 cups of milk
- 1/2 pound heavy cream
- 1/2 cup grated Swiss or Havarti cheese
- A pinch of salt
- Freshly ground black pepper.
- 2 tbsp. butter, sliced into cubes.

Method:

- Use nonstick spray on a 6-by-6-by-2-inch baking pan.
- In a medium mixing bowl, combine the corn, flour, eggs, milk, and light cream. Combine the cheese, salt, and pepper in a mixing bowl.
- Pour this mixture into the baking pan that has been prepared. Make a smear with the butter.
- 15 minutes in the oven

A suggestion for a substitution:

You may replace the frozen corn with one 15-ounce can of drained corn. Alternatively, cut the kernels from 2 to 3 ears of corn to use in this recipe.

Cost per serving:

255 calories; 16 grams of total fat; 10 grams of saturated fat; 87 milligrams of cholesterol; 136 milligrams of sodium, 9g protein; 2g fiber; 21g carbohydrate

DESSERTS RECIPES

GRILLED FRUIT, CURRIED

Preparation time: 10 minutes/Cooking time: 5 minutes/Serves 6 to 8 350°F GRILL

QUICK, GLUTEN-FREE, AND VEGETARIAN:

If you've never tried grilled fruit, this is a great place to start. Grilling caramelizes the sugars in fruits, bringing out their taste and even transforming under ripe fruit into a delicious treat. For a refreshing contrast, serve with sherbet or ice cream.

Ingredients:

- Two ripe peaches
- Two ripe pears
- Two plums
- 2 tbsp. softened butter.
- 1 tablespoon honey
- 2 to 3 tablespoons curry powder

Method:

1. Remove the pits from the peaches and cut each half in half again.
2. Remove the stems from the pears and cut them in half. Each half should be cut in half again. Repeat with the plums.
3. Cover your work area with a thick piece of heavy-duty foil. Arrange the fruit on the foil and sprinkle with the honey and butter. Garnish with curry powder.
4. Wrap the fruit in foil, leaving some room for air in the package.
5. Place the foil packet in the basket and grill for 5 to 8 minutes, shaking once while cooking, until the fruit is soft and tender.

Suggestions for an ingredient:

Pears oxidize quickly when cut, resulting in dark fruit. By squeezing a little fresh lemon juice over the slices, you can keep them from browning. The ascorbic acid in lemon helps fight oxidation.

Cost per serving: 107 calories; 4 grams total fat; 3 grams saturated fat; 10 milligrams cholesterol; 29 milligrams sodium, 1g protein; 3g fiber; 19g carbohydrate

CRISP WITH APPLES, PEACHES, AND CRANBERRIES

Preparation time: 10 minutes/Cooking time: 12 minutes/Serves 8

Preheat the oven to 380°F.

A Vegetarian Family Favorite:

A crisp, also known as a crumble, is a dessert made of cooked fruit and topped with a sweet streusel. This traditional dessert is ideal for autumnal gatherings. Serve with a spoonful of vanilla ice cream or lightly whipped cream.

Ingredients:

- 1 apple, peeled and chopped
- 2 ripe peaches, peeled and chopped
- 1/3 cup dried cranberries
- 2 tablespoons honey
- 1 /3 cup sugar, granulated
- 1/4 cups of flour
- 1/2 cup rolled oats
- 3 tbsp of softened butter.

Method:

Combine the apple, peaches, cranberries, and honey in a 6-by-6-by-2-inch baking dish.

Combine the brown sugar, flour, oats, and butter in a medium mixing basin and whisk until crumbly. This mixture should be sprinkled over the fruit in the pan.

Bake for 10 to 12 minutes, or until the fruit has bubbled and the topping has become golden brown. Serve hot.

A suggestion for a substitution:

This recipe may be modified to include other fruits. Instead of the apples and peaches, use sliced plums or nectarines. Alternatively, in lieu of the dried cranberries, add golden raisins or currants.

Cost per serving:

134 calories; 5 grams of total fat; 3 grams of saturated fat; 11 milligrams of cholesterol; 33 milligrams of sodium, 1g protein; 2g fiber; 23g carbohydrate

CORNMEAL CAKE WITH ORANGE

Preparation time: 7 minutes/Cooking time: 23 minutes/Serves 8

Preheat the oven to 340°F.

A Vegetarian Family Favorite:

This soft cake recipe benefits from the addition of cornmeal, which provides flavor and a hint of bite. When the cake is still hot, an orange glaze is poured over it and soaks into the crumbs. For a morning treat or afternoon snack, serve this cake with a cup of coffee.

Ingredients:

- Flour-based nonstick baking spray
- all-purpose flour (1 1/4 cup)
- 1/3 cup yellow cornmeal
- 3/4 cups of granulated sugar
- 1 teaspoon baking soda
- 1/4 cups of safflower oil
- 1 1/4 cups of orange juice (distributed)
- 1 tsp vanilla extract
- 1/4 cups of granulated sugar

Method:

1. Set aside a 6-by-6-by-2-inch baking sheet sprayed with nonstick spray.
2. In a medium mixing basin, combine the flour, cornmeal, sugar, baking soda, and salt.
3. Mix in the safflower oil, 1 cup of orange juice, and vanilla extract.
4. Place the baking pan in the air fryer and pour the batter in. Bake the cake for 23 minutes, or until a toothpick inserted into the middle comes out clean.
5. Place the cake on a cooling rack after removing it from the basket. Make around 20 holes in the cake using a toothpick.
6. In a small mixing bowl, combine the remaining 1/4 cups of orange juice and the
7. Stir in the powdered sugar well. Drizzle this mixture over the heated cake gently, allowing it to soak.
8. Let it cool fully before cutting into wedges to serve.

What Did You Know? When testing for doneness while baking cakes, there are a few principles to follow. When softly stroked with a finger, a cake should bounce back lightly. Alternatively, stick a clean toothpick into the cake and it should come out clean. Finally, when a cake is done, it begins to gently peel away from the edges of the baking pan.

Cost per serving:

253 calories; 7 grams of total fat; 1 gram of saturated fat; 45 milligrams of cholesterol; 161 milligrams of sodium,45g carbs; 1g fiber; 3g protein

HAND PIES FROM THE BLACK FOREST

Preparation time: 10 minutes/Cooking time: 15 minutes/Serves 6

Preheat the oven to 300°F.

A Vegetarian Family Favorite:

The Black Forest Torte is a traditional cake made with chocolate and cherries. This simple dish is enjoyable to prepare, and children particularly like it. The chocolate and cherries are enveloped in puff pastry that cooks perfectly in the air fryer. These are delicious both warm and cold.

Ingredients:

- 3 tbsp chocolate chips (dark or light)
- 2 tbsp. thick hot fudge sauce.
- 2 tbsp of dried cherries, chopped
- 1 thawed (10-by-15-inch) sheet of puff pastry.
- 1 egg white, beaten
- 2 tablespoons sugar
- 1/2 teaspoons cinnamon powder

Method:

1. Combine the chocolate chips, fudge sauce, and dried cherries in a small bowl.
2. On a floured board, roll out the puff pastry. Using a sharp knife, cut the dough into 6 squares.
3. Fill the middle of each puff pastry square with the chocolate chip mixture. To construct triangles, fold the squares in half. To seal, press the edges firmly with the tines of a fork.
4. Brush the triangles with the beaten egg white on both sides sparingly.
5. Sprinkle some sugar and cinnamon on top.

6. Bake for 15 minutes, or until the triangles are golden brown in the air fryer basket. Because the filling will be hot, let it cool for at least 20 minutes before serving.

A Tip for the Air Fryer:

Make sure these mini pies don't touch in the air fryer so they brown and crisp on all sides.

Cost per serving:

173 calories; 9 grams total fat; 3 grams saturated fat; 1 milligram cholesterol; 62 milligram sodium,3g protein; 1g fiber; 21g carbohydrate

CHEESECAKE WITH MARBLES

Preparation time: 10 minutes/Cooking time: 20 minutes/Serves 8

Preheat the oven to 320°F.

A Vegetarian Family Favorite

A cheesecake baked in an air fryer may sound unlikely, but it works! This cheesecake combines vanilla and chocolate flavors. It's not only wonderful, but it's also stunning. Splurge on this as a dessert after a weeknight dinner.

Ingredients:

- 1 cup graham crackers, crushed
- 3 tbsp of softened butter.
- softened cream cheese,1 1/2 (8-ounce) packets
- 1/3 pound of sugar
- Two beaten eggs
- 1 tablespoon flour
- 1 tsp vanilla extract
- 1/4-cup cocoa syrup

Method:

1. In a small dish, combine the graham cracker crumbs and butter and stir thoroughly. Place it in the freezer to firm the bottom of a 6-by-6-by-2-inch baking pan.
2. In a medium mixing bowl, add the cream cheese and sugar and stir thoroughly. One at a time, beat in the eggs. Mix in the flour and vanilla extract.
3. Transfer 23 cups of the filling to a small mixing dish and whisk in the chocolate syrup until well mixed.

4. Pour the vanilla filling into the crust-lined baking dish. Drop spoonful of the chocolate filling over the vanilla filling. To marbleize the fillings, mix them in a zigzag pattern with a clean butter knife.
5. Bake the cheesecake for 20 minutes, or until it is barely set.
6. Cool for 1 hour on a wire rack before cooling in the refrigerator until the cheesecake is hard.

A suggestion for a substitution:

Other tastes may be created using this basic formula. For a chocolate cheesecake, add 12 cups of chocolate syrup and do not split the batter. For a lemon cheesecake, omit the chocolate syrup and replace it with approximately 134 cups of lemon curd.

Cost per serving:

311 calories; 21 grams total fat; 13 grams saturated fat; 99 milligrams cholesterol; 272 milligrams sodium, 1g fiber; 25g carbohydrate; 6g protein

BROWNIES IN BLACK AND WHITE

Preparation time: 10 minutes; cooking time: 20 minutes; yields 12 brownies.

Preheat the oven to 340°F.

A Vegetarian Family Favorite

Who doesn't like a good brownie? The brownies remain moist and profoundly rich in the air fryer yet have the most amazing crispy and crisp top. This simple dish should soon become a regular part of your air-frying repertoire.

Ingredients:

- One egg
- 1/4 cups of granulated sugar
- 2 tablespoons white sugar
- 2 tablespoons safflower oil
- 1 tsp vanilla extract
- 1/4 tbsp. cocoa powder
- 1/3 cup all-purpose flour
- 1/4-Cup White Chocolate Chippies
- Flour-based nonstick baking spray

Method:

1. In a medium mixing bowl, combine the eggs, brown sugar, and white sugar.
2. Mix in the oil and vanilla extract.
3. Stir in the chocolate powder and flour just until mixed. Incorporate the white chocolate chips.
4. Use nonstick spray on a 6-by-6-by-2-inch baking pan. Pour the brownie batter into the prepared pan.
5. Bake for 20 minutes, or until the brownies are firm to the touch when gently touched with a finger. Allow it to cool for 30 minutes before slicing and serving.

Cooking hint:

Cocoa powder is measured in the same way that flour is: scoop it gently into a measuring cup and level off the top with the back of a knife.

Never scoop flour or dry ingredients into a measuring cup since it adds too much to the recipe and results in thick, heavy cookies, cakes, and bars.

Cost per serving:

81 calories; 4 grams total fat; 1 gram saturated fat; 14 milligrams cholesterol; 10 milligrams sodium, 1g fiber; 11g carbohydrate; 1g protein

CUPCAKES WITH CHOCOLATE AND PEANUT BUTTER GANACHE

TIME TO PREPARE: 10 MINUTES; TIME TO COOK: 10 TO 13 MINUTES; MAKES 8 CUPCAKES

Preheat the oven to 320°F.

A Vegetarian Family Favorite:

Molten cupcakes are slightly under baked cakes with a liquid middle. This recipe is a little unique: Before baking, a ball of peanut butter and powdered sugar is placed in the center of each cupcake. As the cake bakes, it softens, resulting in a molten center of luscious peanut butter. Serve these warm cupcakes with vanilla ice cream.

Ingredients:

- Flour-based nonstick baking spray
- 1 1/3 pound chocolate cake mix (15 oz. box)
- 1 egg
- 1 quail egg yolk
- 1/4 cups of safflower oil

- 1/4 cups of boiling water
- 1/3-cup soured cream
- 3 tablespoons peanut butter
- 1 tbsp. powdered sugar

Method:

1. 16 foil muffin cups may be doubled to produce 8 cups. Set aside. Lightly coat each with nonstick spray.
2. In a medium mixing bowl, add the cake mix, egg, egg yolk, safflower oil, water, and sour cream.
3. In a small mixing dish, combine the peanut butter and powdered sugar. Make eight balls out of this mixture.
4. Fill each muffin cup halfway with chocolate batter and top with a peanut butter ball. To cover the peanut butter balls, spoon the remaining batter on top.
5. Place the cups in the air fryer basket, allowing some space between them. Bake for 10–13 minutes, or until the tops seem dry and firm.
6. Allow the cupcakes to cool for approximately 10 minutes before serving warm.

Suggestions for an ingredient:

Keep the remaining chocolate cake mix in a tightly sealed heavy-duty plastic bag. Be sure to mark it with the date that you used it. Use it within two weeks, preferably to create extra batches of this recipe!

Cost per serving:

195 calories; 15 grams total fat; 3 grams saturated fat; 51 milligrams cholesterol; 158 milligrams sodium, 1g fiber; 13g carbohydrate; 4g protein

BREAD PUDDING WITH CHOCOLATE AND PEANUT BUTTER

Preparation time: 10 minutes/Cooking time: 10 to 12 minutes/Serves 8

Preheat the oven to 330°F.

A Vegetarian Family Favorite

Bread pudding is the quintessential comfort dish. The addition of chocolate and peanut butter to this recipe provides a subtle richness and amplifies the taste. Serve with rich whipped cream to add to the opulence.

Ingredients:

- Flour-based nonstick baking spray
- One egg
- 1 quail egg yolk
- Cocoa milk (3/4 cups)
- 2 tablespoons cocoa powder
- 3 tbsp brown sugar
- three tablespoons of peanut butter
- 1 tsp vanilla extract
- 5 cubed slices of firm white bread.
- Nonstick spray a 6-by-6-by-2-inch baking pan.

Method:

In a medium mixing bowl, add the egg, egg yolk, chocolate milk, cocoa, brown sugar, peanut butter, and vanilla extract. Allow the bread cubes to soak for 10 minutes.

Fill the prepared pan halfway with this mixture. Bake for 10 to 12 minutes, or until the pudding is set.

A suggestion for a substitution:

You may use a variety of breads in this dish. You may use cubed doughnuts or a fast bread like banana bread or peanut butter bread instead.

Cost per serving:

102 calories; 5 grams total fat; 2 grams saturated fat; 50 milligrams cholesterol; 90 milligrams sodium,1g fiber; 11g carbohydrate; 4g protein

A LARGE CHOCOLATE CHIP COOKIE

Preparation time: 7 minutes/Cooking time: 9 minutes/Serves 4

Preheat the oven to 300°F.

VEGETARIAN, FAMILY FAVORITE, AND QUICK

Chocolate chip cookies are a favorite among many people. But have you ever attempted to make one that is 6 inches in diameter? This entertaining recipe yields one large cookie that feeds four people. Everyone takes a bite to savor. This cookie is extremely delicious when served warm.

Ingredients:

- Flour-based nonstick baking spray
- 3 tbsp of softened butter.
- 1 tablespoon brown sugar plus 1/3 cup brown sugar
- 1 quail egg yolk
- 1/2 cups of all-purpose flour
- 2 tbsp. white chocolate powder.
- 1/4 tsp baking soda
- 1/2 tsp vanilla extract
- one-quarter cup chocolate chips

Method:

1. In a medium mixing bowl, cream together the butter and brown sugar until creamy.
2. Stir in the egg yolk.
3. Mix in the flour, white chocolate, baking soda, and vanilla extract.
4. Add the chocolate chips and stir well.
5. Using parchment paper, line a 6-by-6-by-2-inch baking sheet. Using a nonstick baking spray with flour, coat the parchment paper.
6. Spread the batter evenly in the prepared pan, leaving a 1/2-inch border all around.
7. Bake for 9 minutes, or until the cookie is light golden and just set.
8. Allow the pan to cool for 10 minutes after removing it from the air fryer. Remove the cookie from the pan, peel off the parchment paper, and place on a wire rack to cool.

A suggestion for a substitution:

Other varieties of chocolate chips may also be used in this recipe. Consider using milk chocolate chips or butterscotch chips. Or add approximately 14 cup chopped pecans or cashews when you whisk in the chocolate chips.

Cost per serving:

309 calories; 22 grams total fat; 14 grams saturated fat; 84 milligrams cholesterol; 178 milligrams sodium,5g protein; 2g fiber; 49g carbohydrate

A Peanut Butter Frosted Cookie

Time to Preparation: 10 Minutes/Time to Cook: 10 Minutes/Serves 4

BAKE AT 310 °F

A Vegetarian Family Favorite

On a weeknight, a large peanut butter cookie covered with melted chocolate is the ideal treat. For an indulgent treat, eat this cookie warm while the icing is still soft.

Ingredients:

- 3 tablespoons of room temperature butter.
- 1 tablespoon brown sugar plus 1/3 cup brown sugar
- 1 quail egg yolk
- 2/3 cup flour
- 5 tbsp of peanut butter (divided)
- 1/4 tsp of baking soda
- 1 tsp vanilla extract
- SEMISWEET CHOCOLATE COOKIES 1/2 CUP

Method:

1. In a medium mixing bowl, cream together the butter and brown sugar until creamy.
2. Stir in the egg yolk.
3. Mix in the flour, 3 tablespoons of peanut butter, baking soda, and vanilla extract.
4. Using parchment paper, line a 6-by-6-by-2-inch baking sheet.
5. Spread the batter evenly in the prepared pan, leaving a 1/2-inch border all around.
6. Bake for 7–10 minutes, or until the cookie is light brown and just set.
7. Allow the pan to cool for 10 minutes after removing it from the air fryer. Remove the cookie from the pan, peel off the parchment paper, and place it on a wire rack to cool.
8. Combine the chocolate chips and the remaining 2 tablespoons of peanut butter in a small heatproof cup. Bake for 1–2 minutes, or until the chips are completely melted. Stir everything together and put it on the cookie.

A tip for a variation:

This recipe may be doubled or tripled. You may alternatively serve the cookie unfrosted or make a frosting with 2 teaspoons of soft butter, 2 tablespoons of peanut butter, and 1/2 cups of powdered sugar.

<u>Cost per serving:</u> 481 calories; 28 grams total fat; 13 grams saturated fat; 75 milligrams cholesterol; 239 milligrams sodium

8g protein; 3g fiber; 52g carbohydrate

Printed in Great Britain
by Amazon

80559779R00072